Preface

The idea for this book came when I was making an anthology of my writing for my children. While doing this, I found lots of artwork that I had produced over the years. I decided to collect the art and compose short poems to accompany each work. Hope Shines Through was born!

The book is divided into four sections. The first is called visiting places. I have travelled to Nicaragua and Ecuador numerous times performing medical service for poor, indigenous or underserved peoples with colleagues. The travel section also has a poem about my ancestral homeland: Puerto Rico.

The section on reminiscing childhood features works that tell the story of my childhood home, my personal interests as a child, a work photoshopped by my son, and poems and artwork about boy scout camp. Scout camp was a big part of my childhood, as well my boys' childhood.

The third section on sharing faith has artwork designed to tell the stories of Eve, Adam, Moses, Chanukah, Christmas, Jonah, and Lehi. From different faith traditions, these stories have motivated the artwork.

Love Everlasting is the last section dedicated to my best friend and the love of my life Moraima. We have been married for 24 years at the time of this printing, and she continues to guide and inspire me.

There are five works in this book that were not completely done by the author. The first "White Birch" was made from a painting my sister, Nilda Keetch, made when she was a teenager. I took a picture of the work, and photoshopped in the colors. The second is called the Waiting Room. My son Pablo Rodríguez did all of the photoshop work. The third one, Eve and Adam, has a snake that was originally painted by my sister, and was transferred to the work.

This book is a work of love. I am thrilled to present it to you and hope that it will be a means to inspire you. May you find the joy that comes from sharing something you create, and from using your means to make a difference for others.

Happy reading!

José E Rodríguez MD, FAAFP

P.D. Many of these works have been published previously in HEAL--Humanism Evolving through Arts and Literature, a journal I co-founded and edited for many years, now in its 11th year of publication

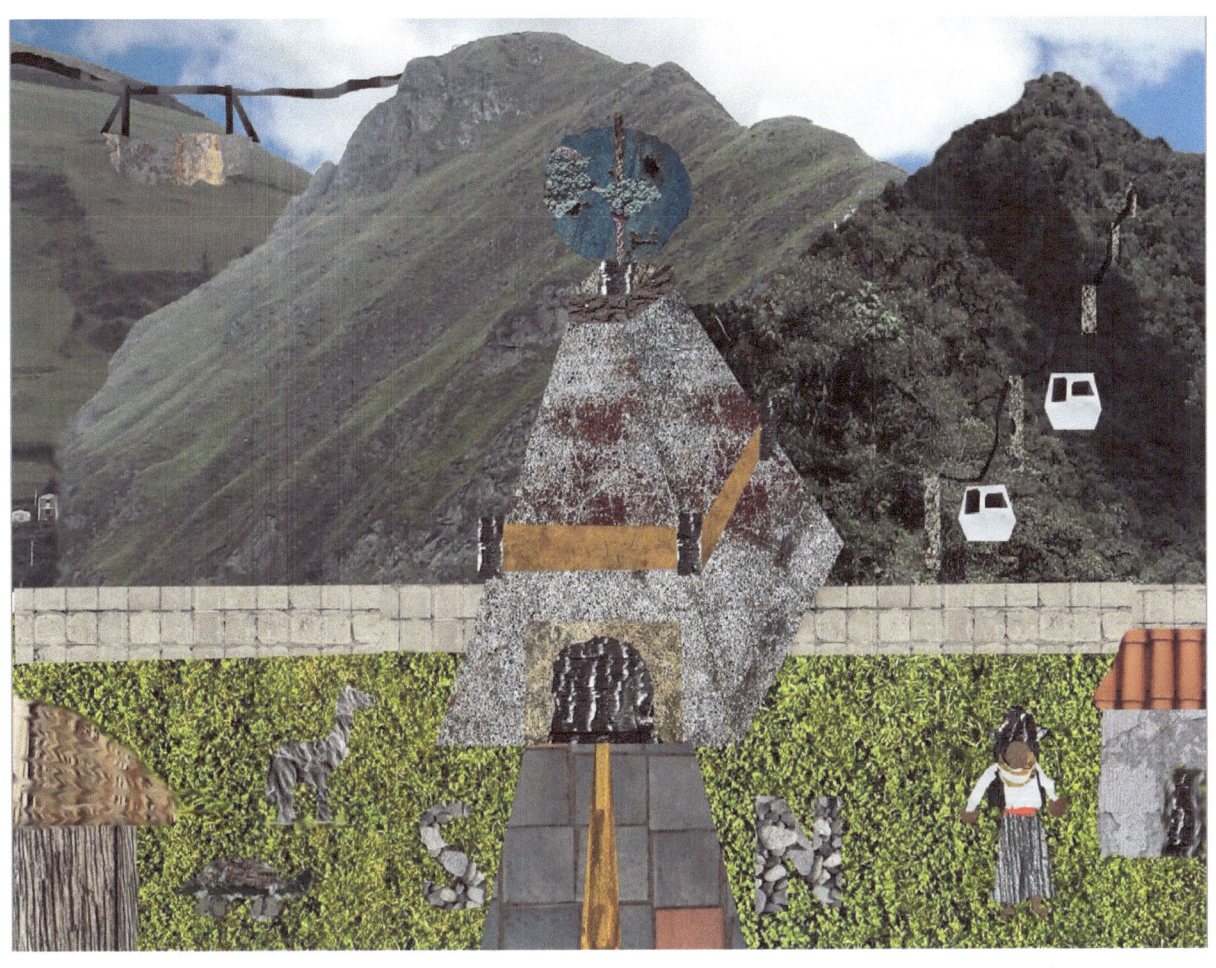

Visiting Places

The best part of travel is meeting new people, or better yet, catching up with those you have not seen.

Service Learning in Nicaragua

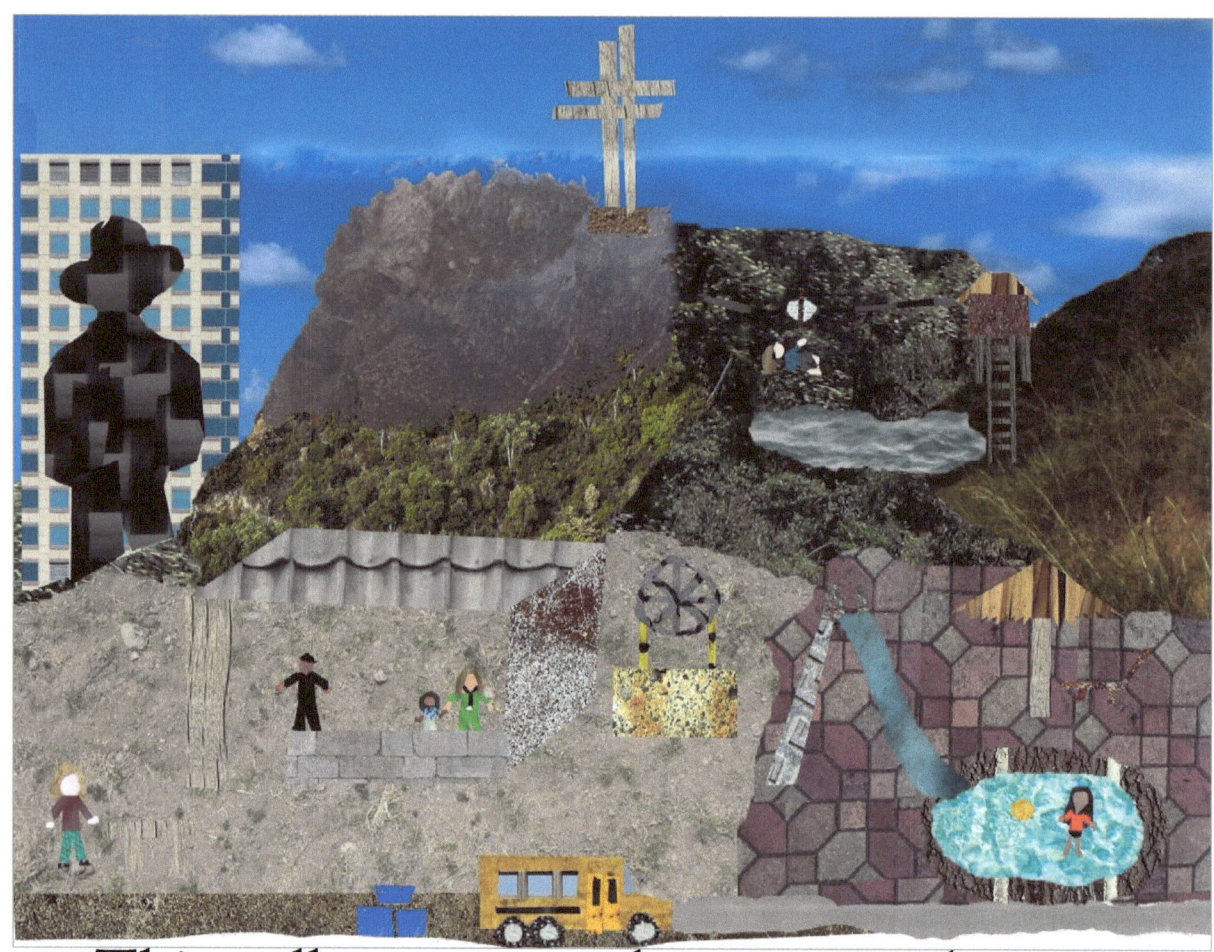

This collage was made to remember our service learning in Nicaragua. We went from place to place in an old school bus and kept our medical supplies in blue containers. The wells had large wheels, with small cups on them to bring up the water. We saw many shadow sculptures of Augusto Cesar Sandino, and in our free time, we swam, zip lined, and visited volcanoes.

Hundreds of patients
Sporadic primary care
Million-pede

Pool dueling monkeys
Tortillas and beans
Running

Mis priced missed flights
Direct to Miami
Welcome home

Ecuador

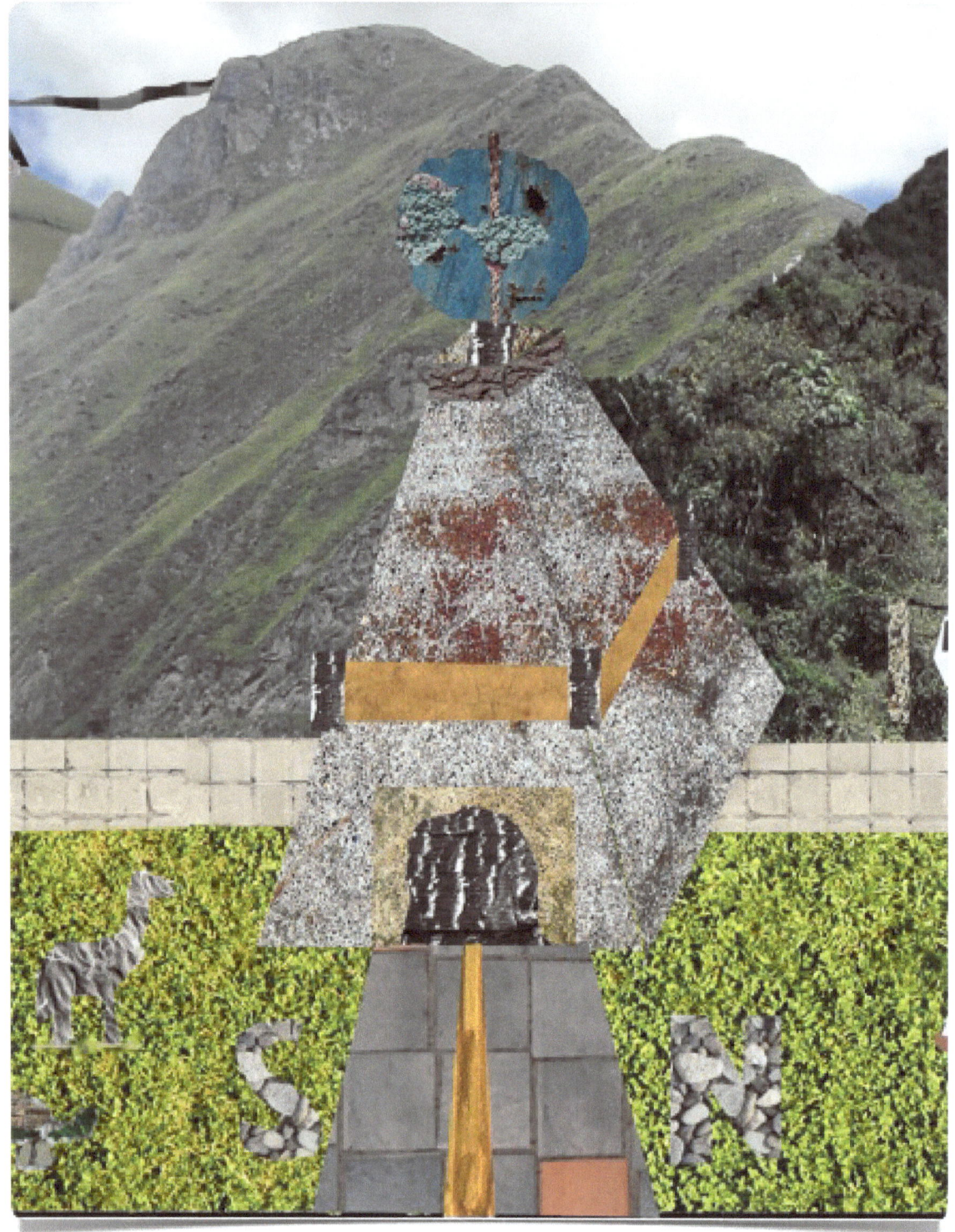

This represents the many times I have visited the ancestral homeland of my wife and children.

Sometimes we saw our family and sometimes we saw our friends

Every time we saw patients, we learned service never ends

We worked with indigenous people who didn't Spanish

But tried to communicate; we must have seemed garish

We saw many others who could not read

We tried to help them because they were in need

After seeing patients, and serving the poor

The students relaxed, and we took a tour

Observing monuments and cities in the beautiful countryside

Although it was very long, we were impressed by the ride

The best part of visiting Ecuador, was seeing our families

Who had lived in the highlands of the Andes

For over seven centuries

Fiesta de Alausí

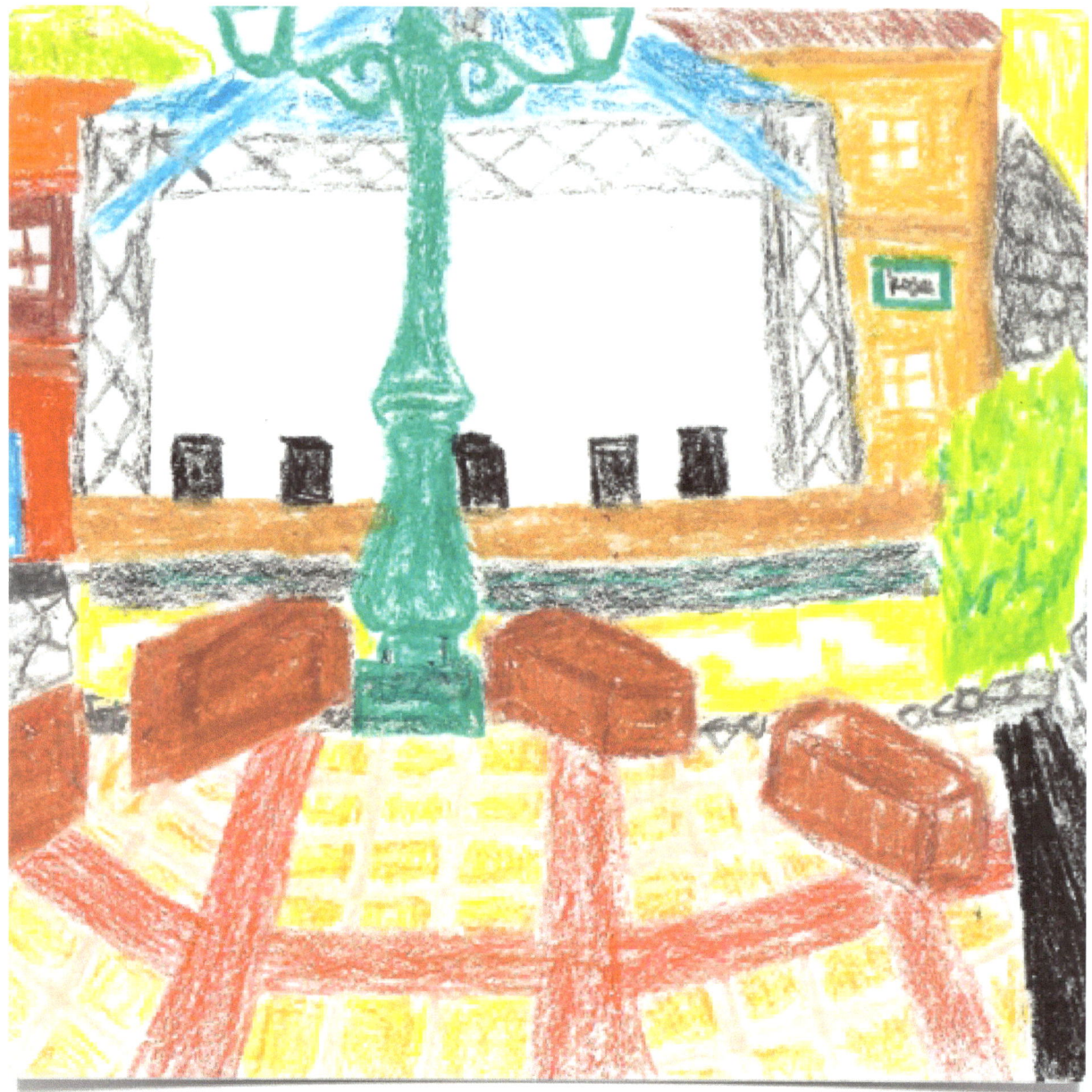

Drawn while staring at the stage. Every year we went to Ecuador, we performed medical service at and around Alausí. It is a small town that has a big party to celebrate the Spanish settlement of the area. It is called the Fiesta de San Pedro de Alausí. This is the stage where invited artists would sing.

Alausí is a paradise in the northern Andes

We would go there every year, and we would bring candies

For the elderly people at the *Hogar de Ancianos*

Delighted to see them, even though we're not *santos*

We gave candy to people who were sick with diabetes

We wanted to brighten their day with lots of sweeties

After the visit we attended a big party

With food and dancing; it was really quite hearty

The stage would later fill with many great acts

It was all paid for with our sales tax

TeléfériQo

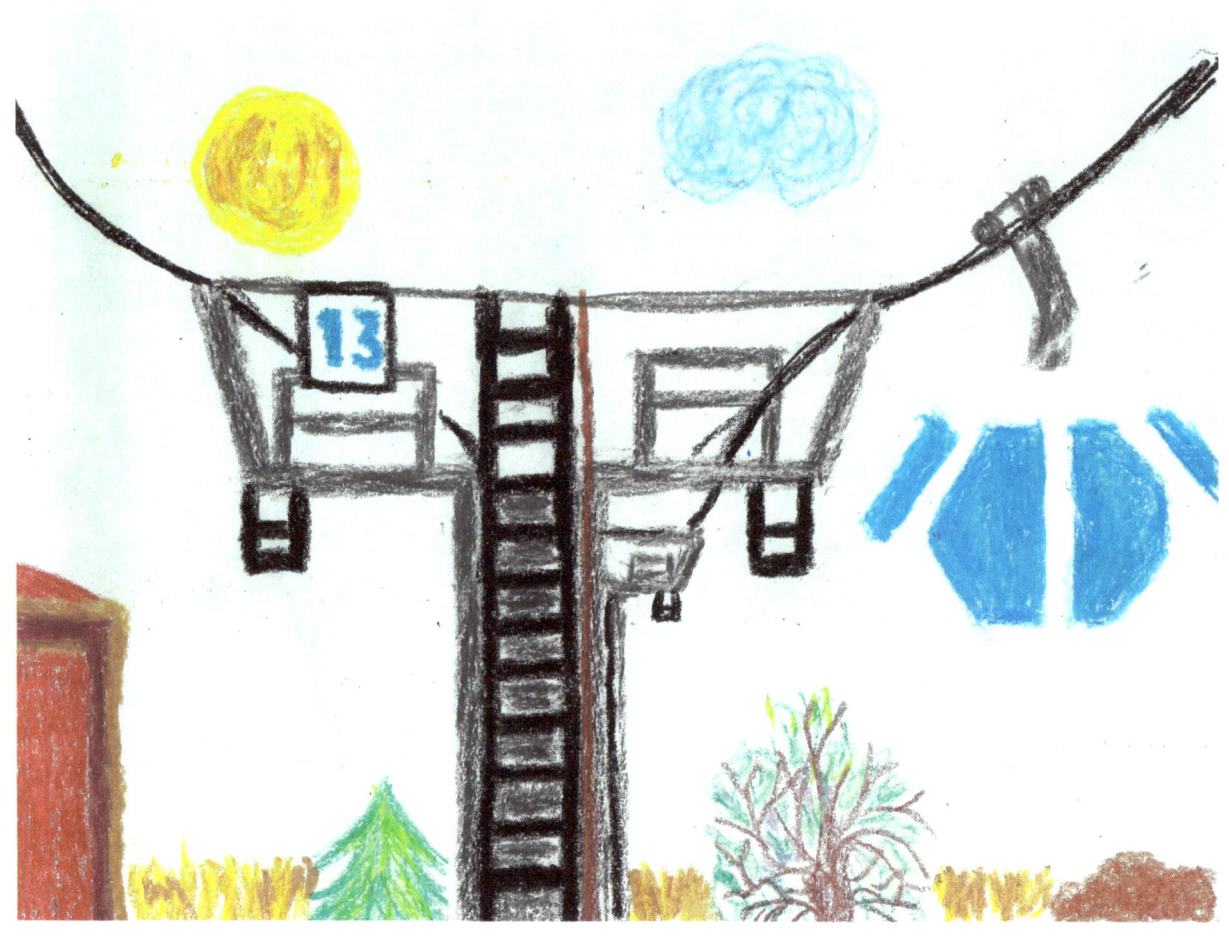

This is my interpretation of the view from cable car that takes people to a 14,000-foot peak as it rises overlooking Quito, Ecuador. It used to give me severe vertigo, but after taking students there for over 10 years, it doesn't seem so scary anymore.

The Teleferiqo is large and it is quite scary

You get in a small car that starts to carry

Up 1000 meters from where you got on

The trip is straight up, so you'd better hold on

You see the ground below that gets farther with each second

You wish is was over, because its longer that you reckoned.

But the view is breathtaking when you disembark

Feelings of fear dissipate after the inauspicious start

You gaze into a valley of over two million people

Everything looks so small, like the top of a tall steeple

That you see from the ground when you squint your eyes

The distance hides people's hates, fears, and lies

That beautiful valley when seen from above

Fills your heart with wonder, with awe and with love

A Puerto Rican Beach Before the Storm

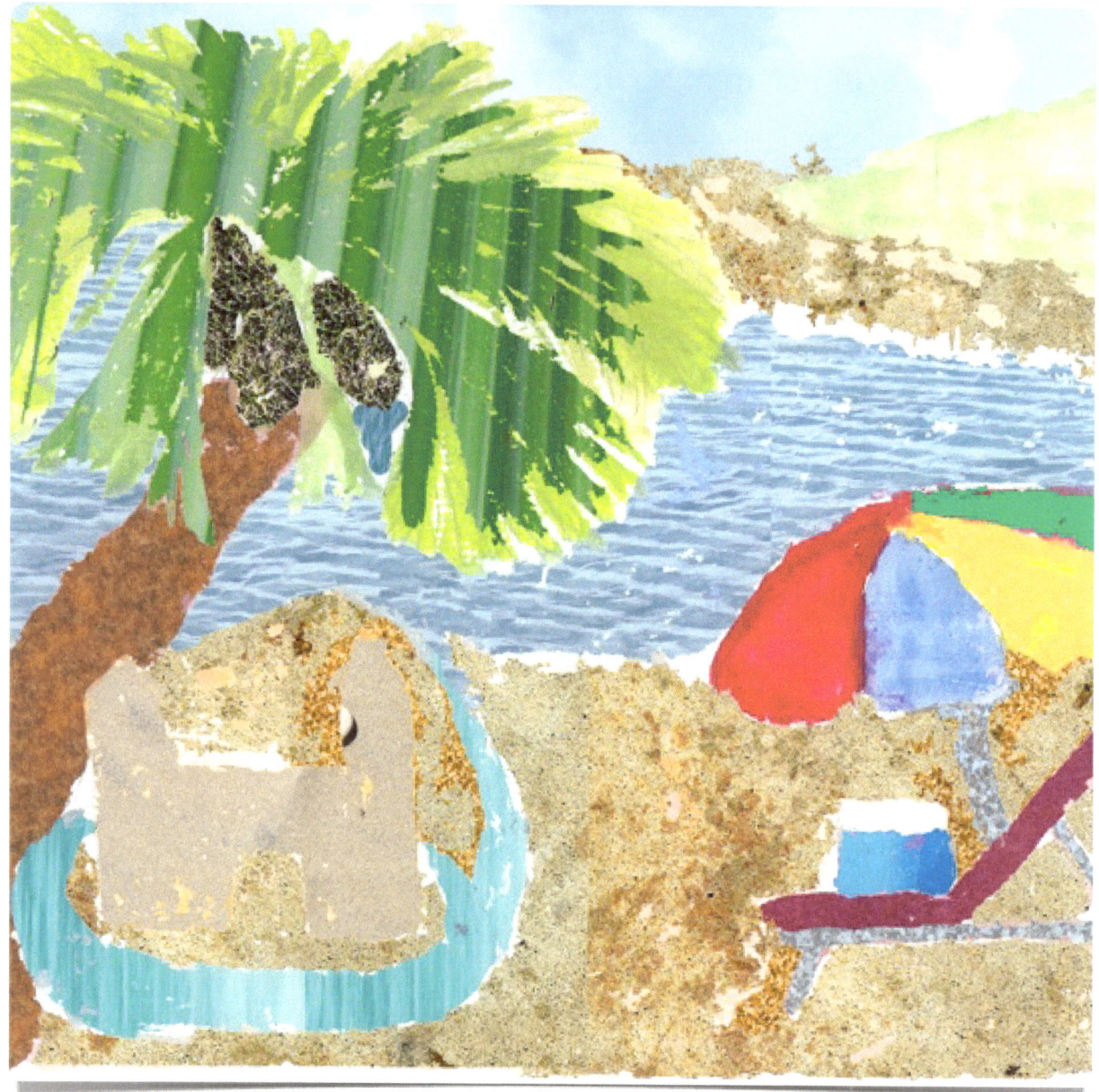

This is mixed media—watercolor and textures from a free, online source. It is based on a beach near my grandmother's home in San Sebastián de las Vegas del Pepino. The beach is called Crashboat, and we visit it every time I go to Puerto Rico

The most beautiful people in the world
The most beautiful beaches in the world
The most beautiful land in the world
Are found in Puerto Rico

Beauty is not enough to get the work done
After the last hurricanes it has not been fun
To clean up mess with little federal aid
So everyone pitched in, and few got paid

Puerto Rico has survived and will again wait
Until the power is on, and the rhetoric dissipates
We can't do anything from here but pray
And hope tomorrow will be better than today

Reminiscing Childhood

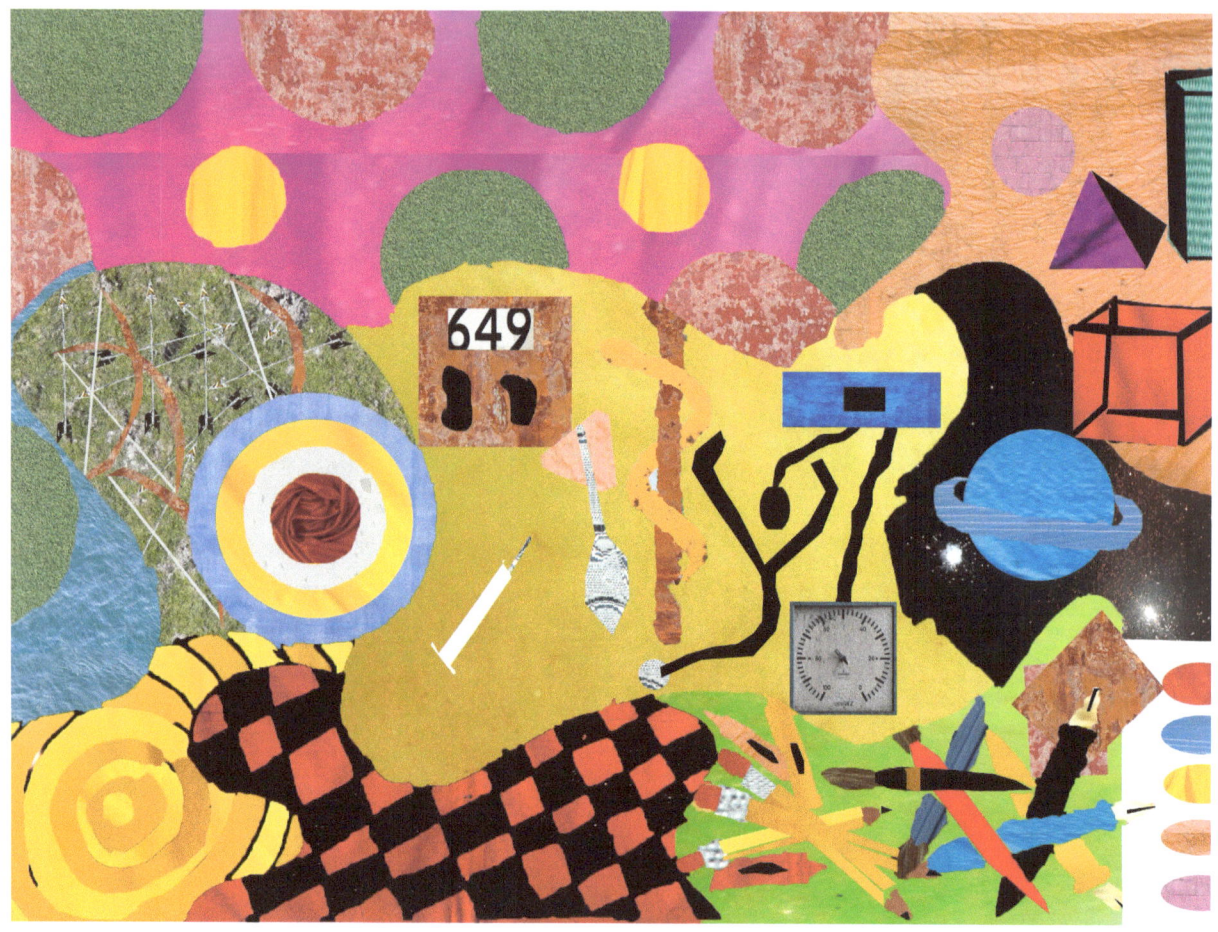

When I was a kid, I loved art, and science and archery and geometry. It's all here in this collage. I drew it when I was in middle school, but photoshopped it just a few years ago.

Marlborough

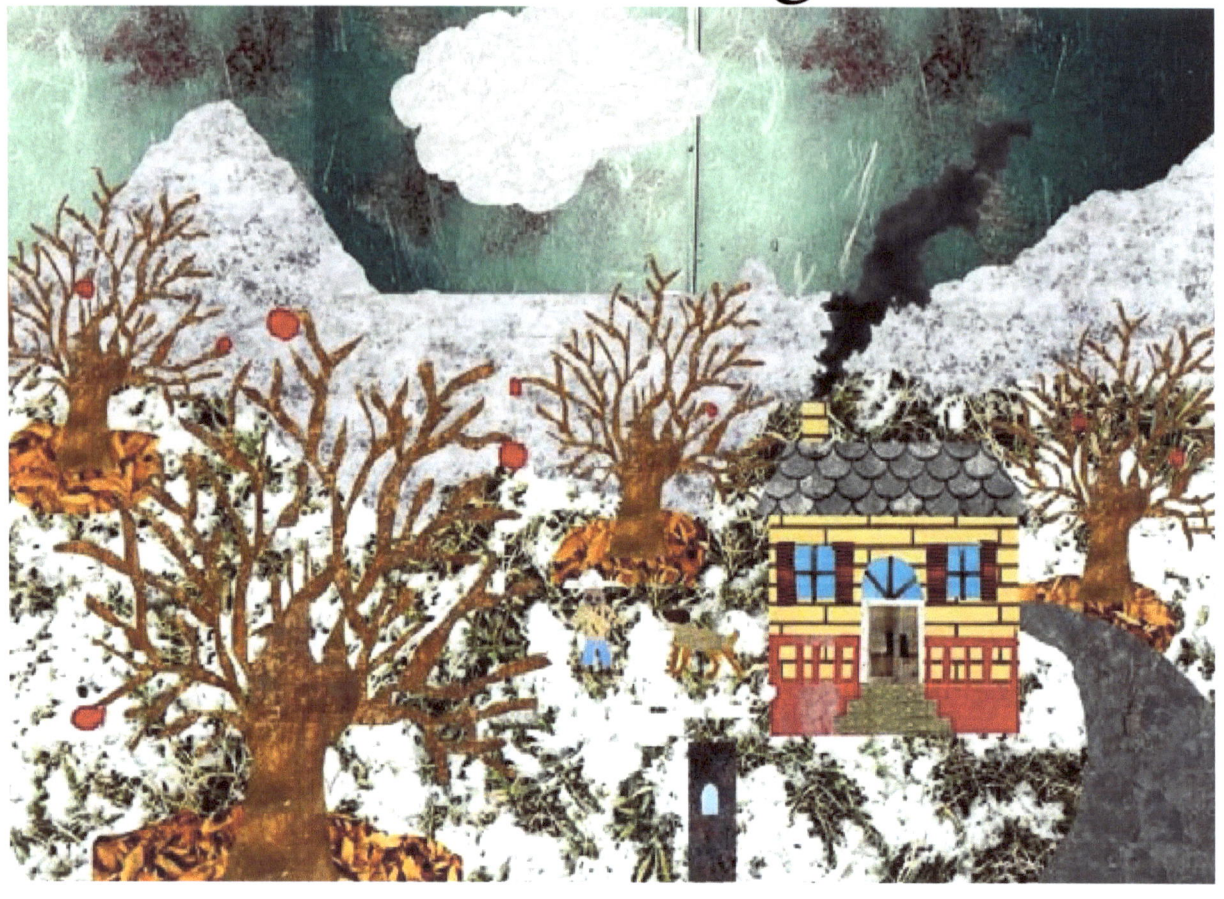

My family and I lived in this house from 1976-1984. I remember learning how to work while I was there, and I do remember having fun. We had a paper route, and my younger brother Juan would help with it. He was 10 years old—and it was a huge help, or a big favor. He didn't have to do it, but without him and my Dad, we could not have gotten all of those papers delivered. I think there were 72 homes, and we made about 35 cents per home, per week.

It looks like a town out of a fairly tale

Marlborough was a sleepy hamlet paced slow as a snail

We lived there as a family until I was fourteen

Even today, I have yet to live anywhere as clean

I worked hard while I lived there at my house and school

Looking back, I didn't even care if I was "cool"

We raised animals, weeded the garden and delivered newspapers

And depended on my dad and my brothers to do me favors

So that I could get my work done

And occasionally, rarely, could have some fun

The White Birch

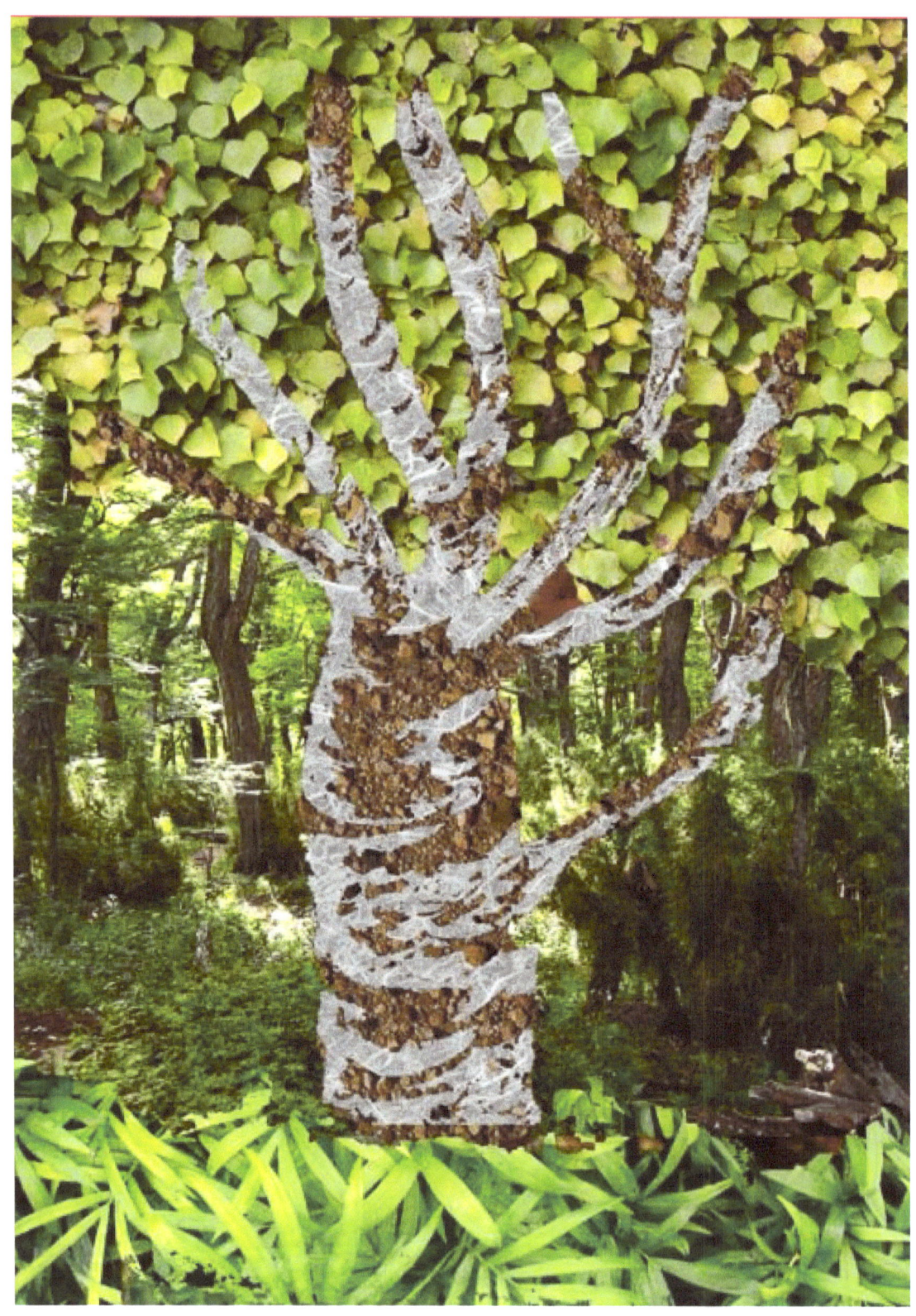

This tree was in front of my childhood home

It was the place that all of us kids would all come

To play with the leaves, or my toys by the trees

And I lost many things, as if I had sneezed

Blowing all of them away in the blink of an eye

When I could not find them I would cry and cry

But I loved that birch tree because it was all white

And if my mom would let me I would play all night

With the bark of that tree which was paper thin

That covered the secrets the white birch held within.

Still Life

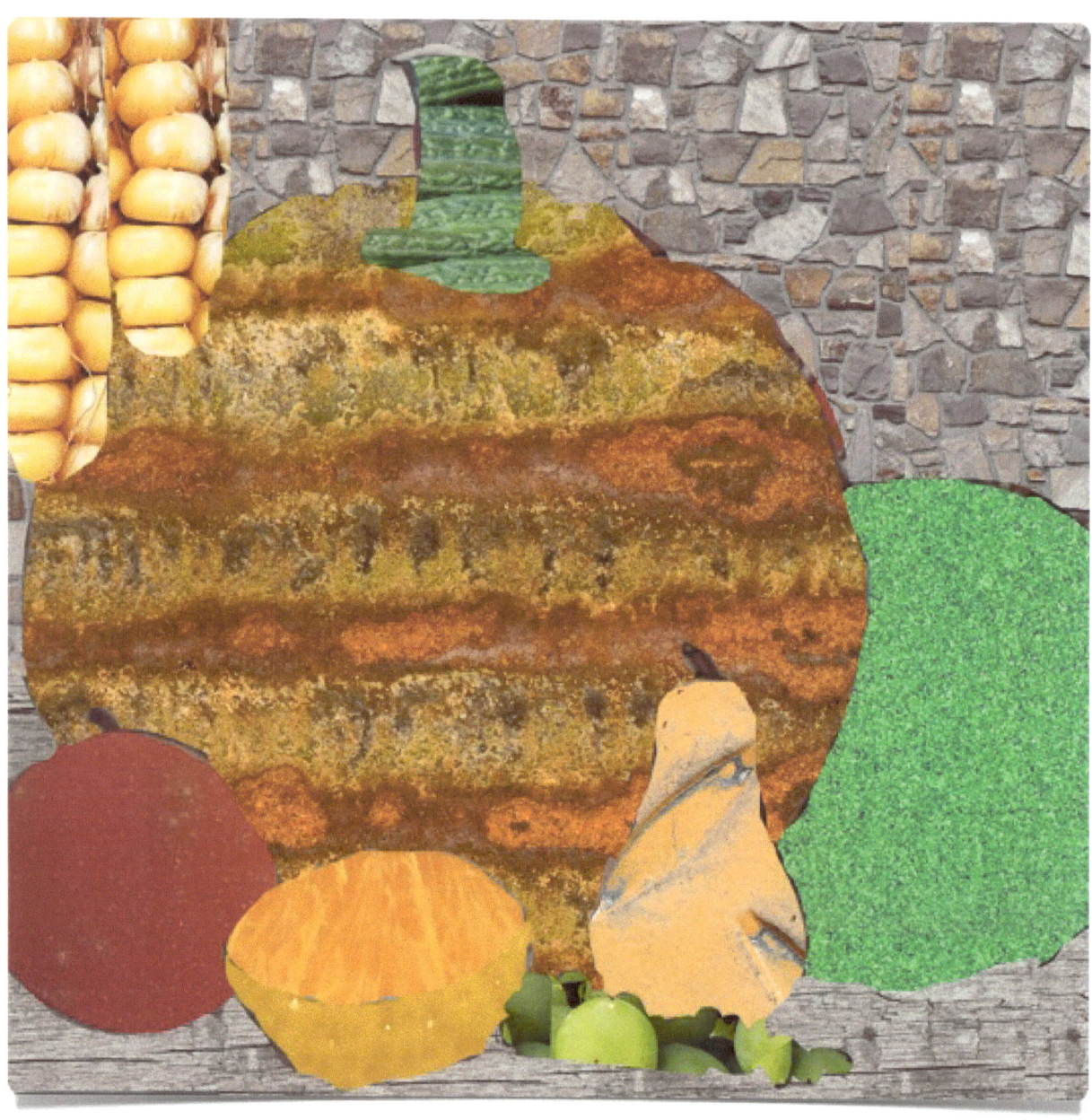

This is a photoshopped version of a work I did in crayon when I was 13. It won 1st place for my age group at the Museum of the Hudson Highlands in Cornwall-on-Hudson, New York. I wonder if the museum is still there....

I wanted to be an artist when I was a kid

My parents got me an art book, and draw I did

Every picture in the book, in pencil and crayon

This one I did often, and I eventually did act on

That dream of being an artist

I finally finished one that I thought I could submit

To a local contest, I wanted that bit

Of fame, and yes, fortune from winning a prize

But I didn't know then, and I didn't realize

That winning did not make me an artist.

Hope Shines

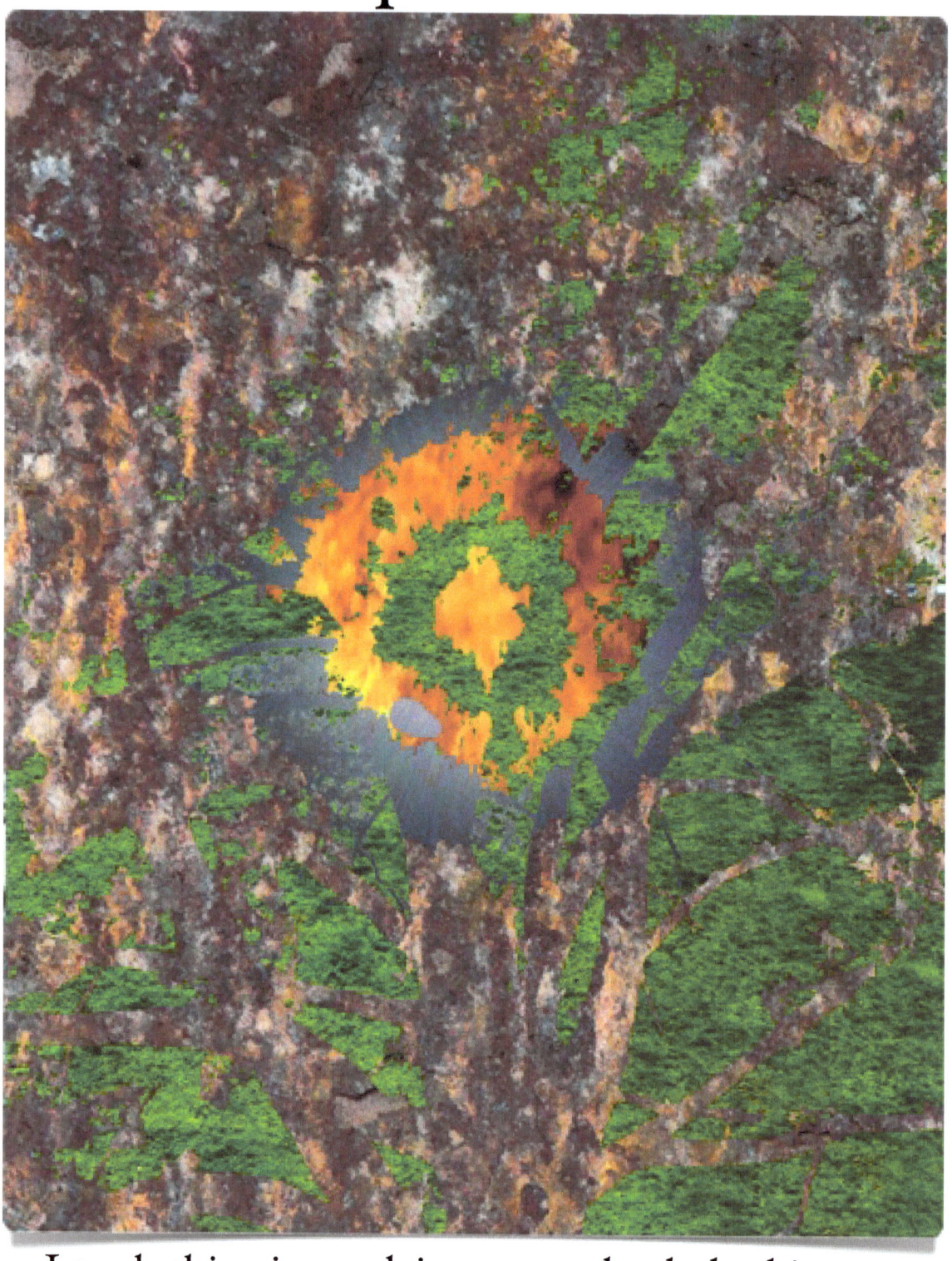

I took this picture lying on my back, looking up
through the branches of a tree at the sun.

Lying down in the grass looking up at the sky

I saw many tree branches protecting my eyes

From the sun's strong rays as they showered the earth

And gave life to everything, representing new birth

My mind wandered to birth and what it means to me

To participate in life--caring for people, and even trees

It became clear to my mind that the sun was a force

Of life and of energy and also the source

Of hope for all people because every day

No matter how bad the past, it is whisked away

When the sun emerges from darkness and it crosses the sky

It helps us see clearly to let past problems die

The Waiting Room

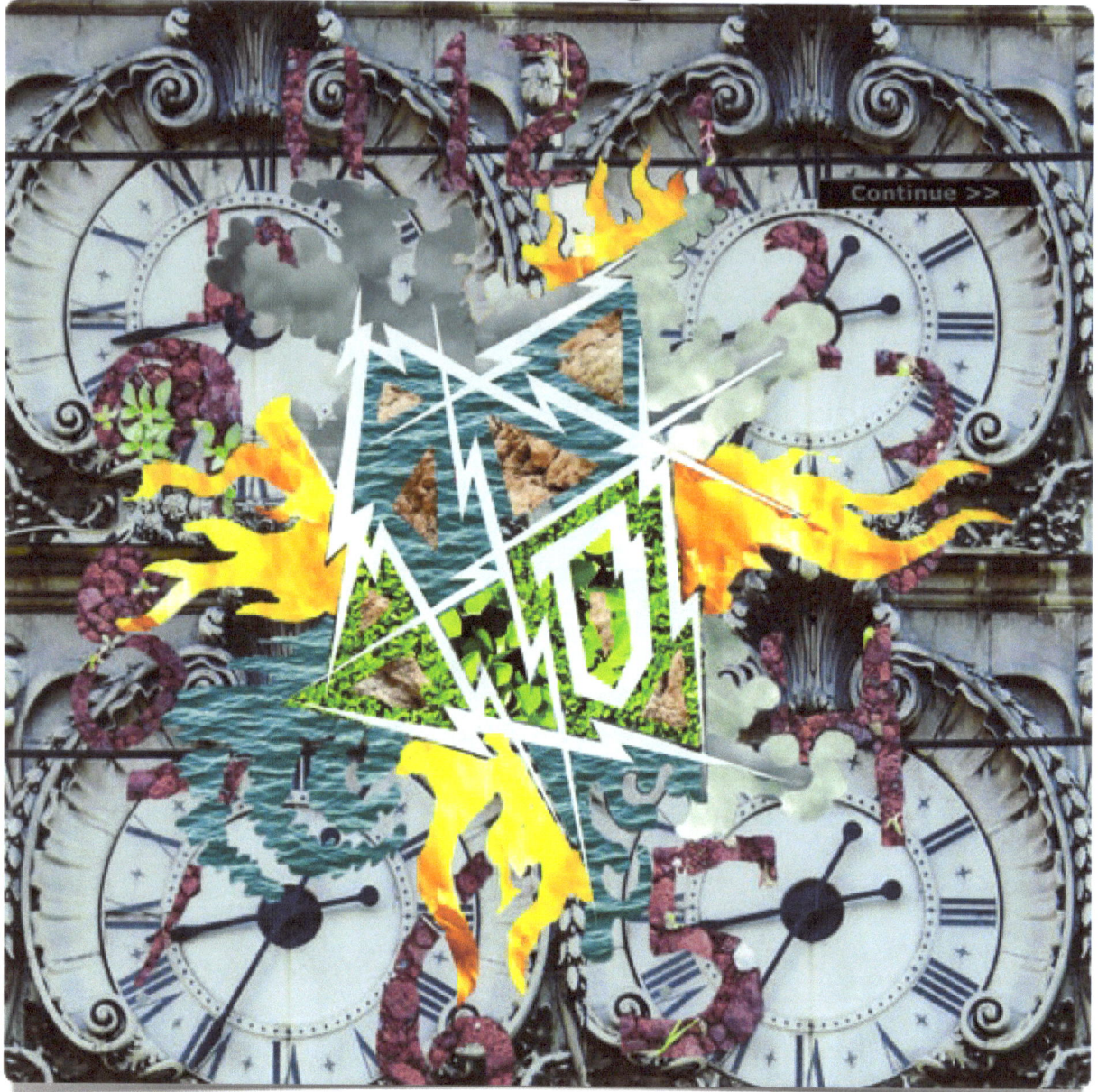

This piece is based on a sketch a patient gave me after waiting for hours to see me. He said I could do whatever I wanted with it, so my son Pablo photoshopped it. A version of this work was featured on the cover of *Family Medicine, November 2013.*

When you have no money, you can't choose how long you wait

To see a doctor, who likely stands at the gate

Of a health care system that doesn't serve you well

Because you may be broke, and may be living in hell

But even in circumstances that are really bad

You can create a drawing even though you are mad

For waiting so long to see an overworked doctor

But you know she appreciates you even though you mocked her

For making you wait so long

Scout Camp

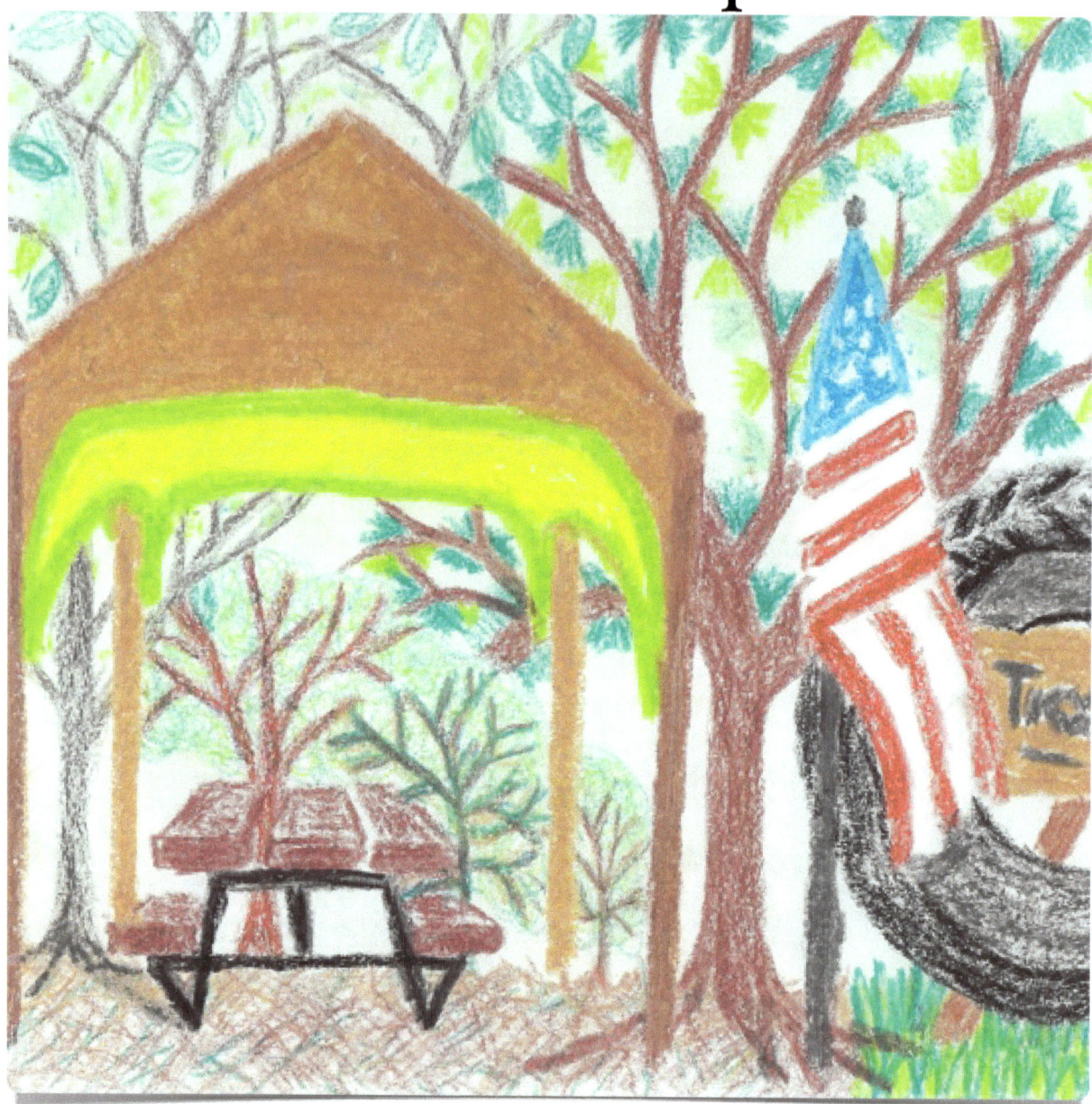

I used oil pastels to make this one, although it looks like it was crayon. My job, as an adult leader at scout camp, was to help the scouts go to their classes. That left me time to draw. This, and the following two pieces were composed when we were at camp.

I made this drawing of our campsite at scout camp

It was in Northern Georgia, where it is *always* damp

My job was to make sure the scouts all went to class

But many of them, like me, would have rather passed

On some of the activities that we did out of doors

The kids preferred air-conditioned houses with floors

To lie on and watch TV or play video games

I guess that the times really have not changed

Lean-to

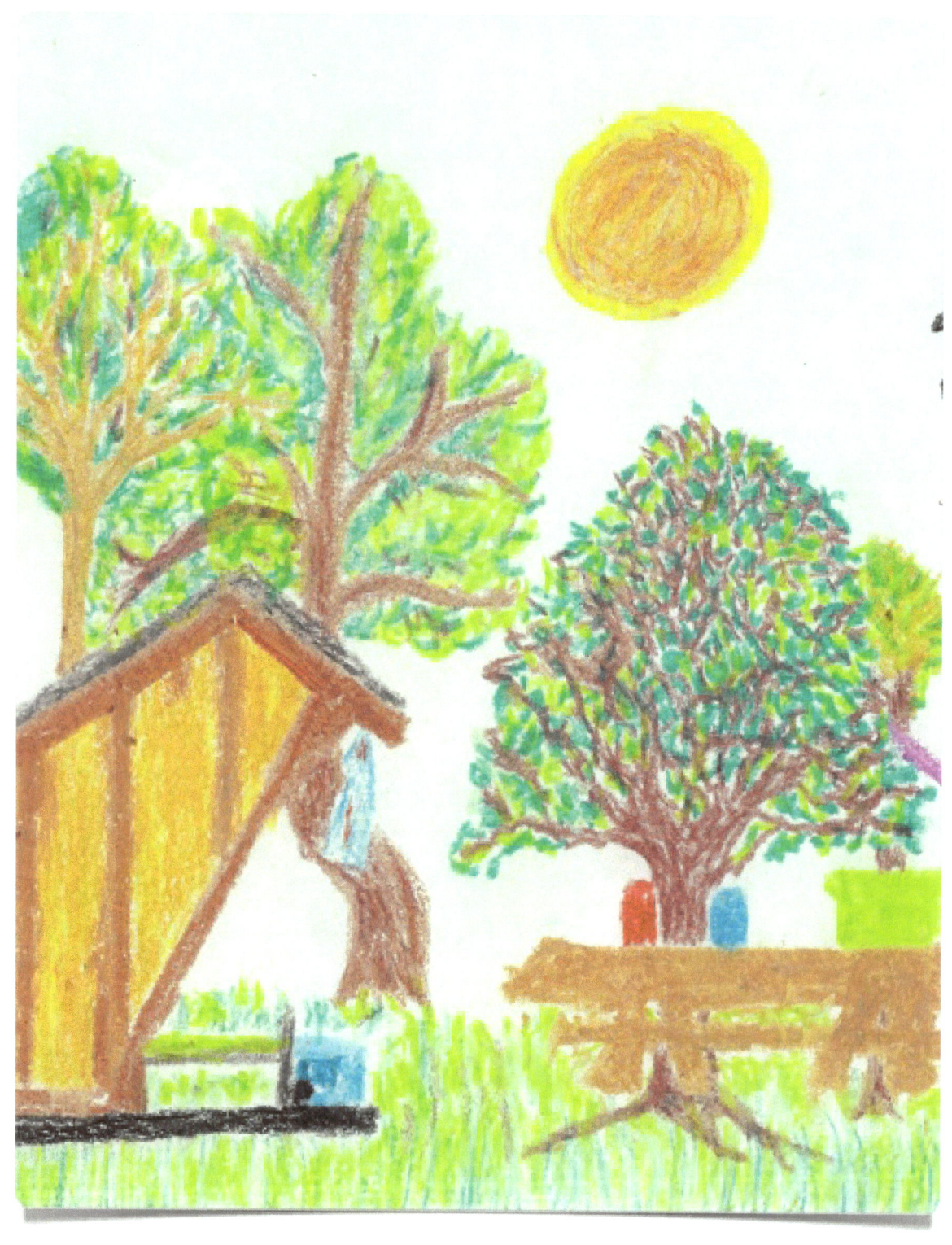

Camping with teenagers is usually fun

Especially when the camping is done

We pack all of our stuff and we get back in the truck

We are home before dark if we have any luck

Although we are served with great food in the mess hall

The scouts usually prefer junk food which is bad for us all

There are many times when we were returning home

That our scouts thought the hour would never come

To eat a home cooked meal and give a hug to their mom

But they wouldn't admit that their home was "the bomb"

They usually puked once or twice in the week

But these are the secrets that we don't dare speak

If we did say a word, we wouldn't know what to do

Because our wives and our moms would forbid a return

To the lean-to.

Camping by the Creek

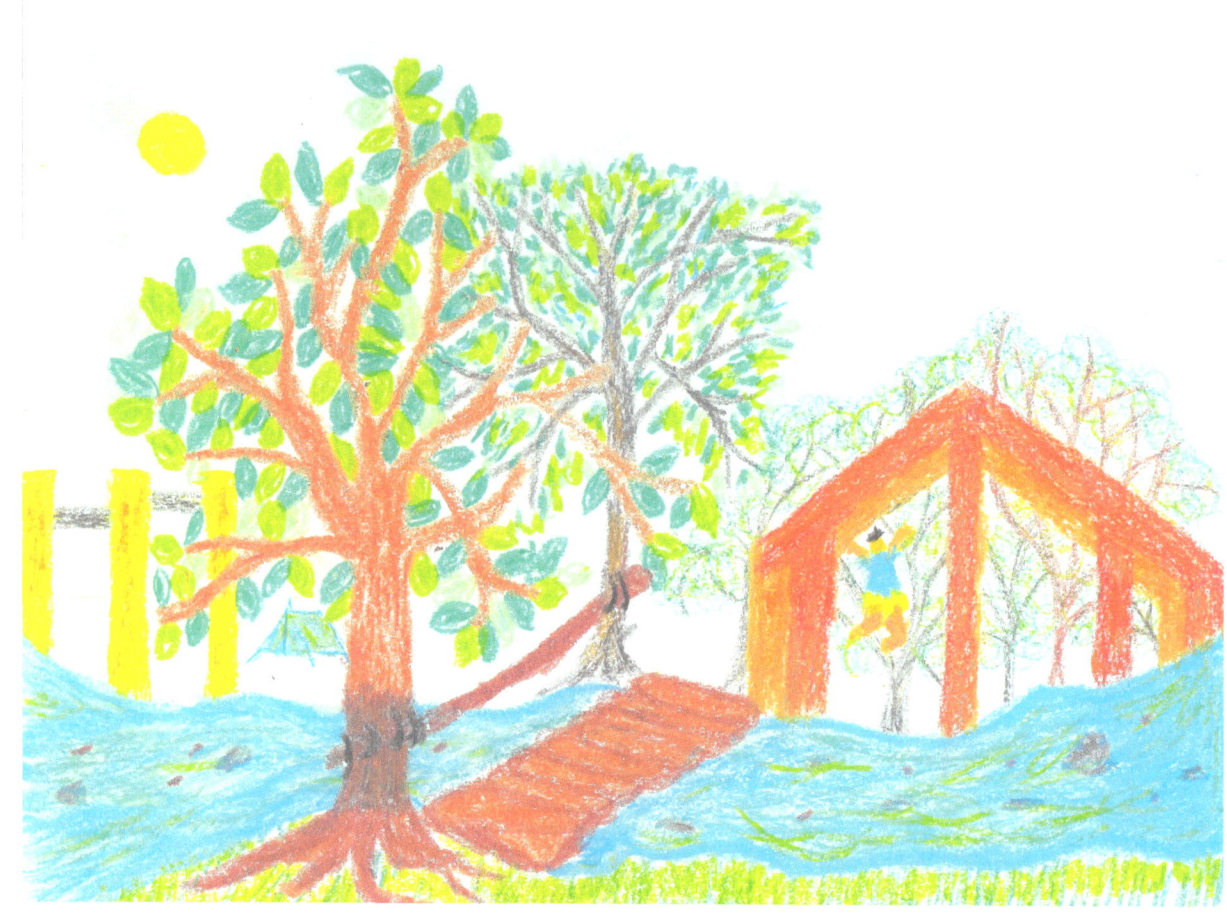

This was at Camp Woodruff. The camp was sponsored by Coca-Cola and had the nicest facilities of any place we had ever camped. However, it was still outside, in the summer heat, in the Southern United States.

My last experience at camp was sponsored by Coca-Cola

The kids were very happy--they were far from Pensacola

From the heat and the bugs and the daily sweat bath

And here all they wanted was to play and get cash

To spend at the scout shop where they could get candy

Without their moms here, they could pretend to be handy

With pocketknives and fishing poles and other manly toys

That's what scout camp is for, to make men out of boys

The creek had cool water and a small wooden bridge

Water so cold you could use it as a fridge

To keep your soda cold that you got from the scout store

But it would likely get drank, and we would always need more

A scout became fond of the local monkey bars

So, he used them all day, till we came home in our cars.

A.D.D.

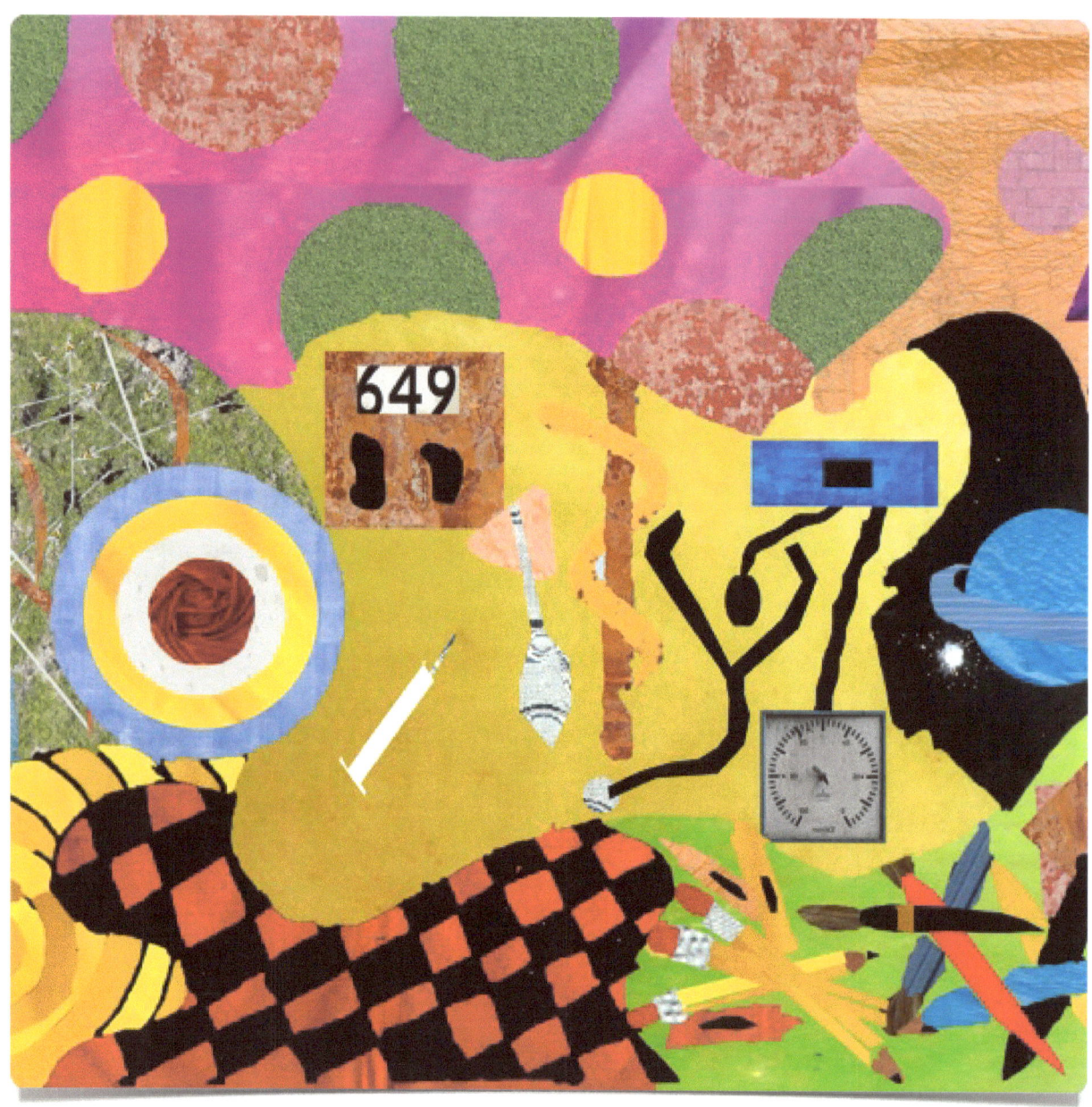

Being everywhere and nowhere, all at the same time. This poem is autobiographical.

Varied interests take me many places at a time

I find myself using time that is not mine

To work on projects from varied interests

And then try to sell them by posting on Pintrest.

I like science and art and poetry and crayons

And writing cool stories and I could go on and on

I have a million thoughts at once and a short attention span

And I lose interest quickly even though I can

Be more creative than most and do a lot more work

But because of ADD I seem like a jerk

Because I'm not always paying attention--

Even though that is not my intention.

Latina Tinker-bell

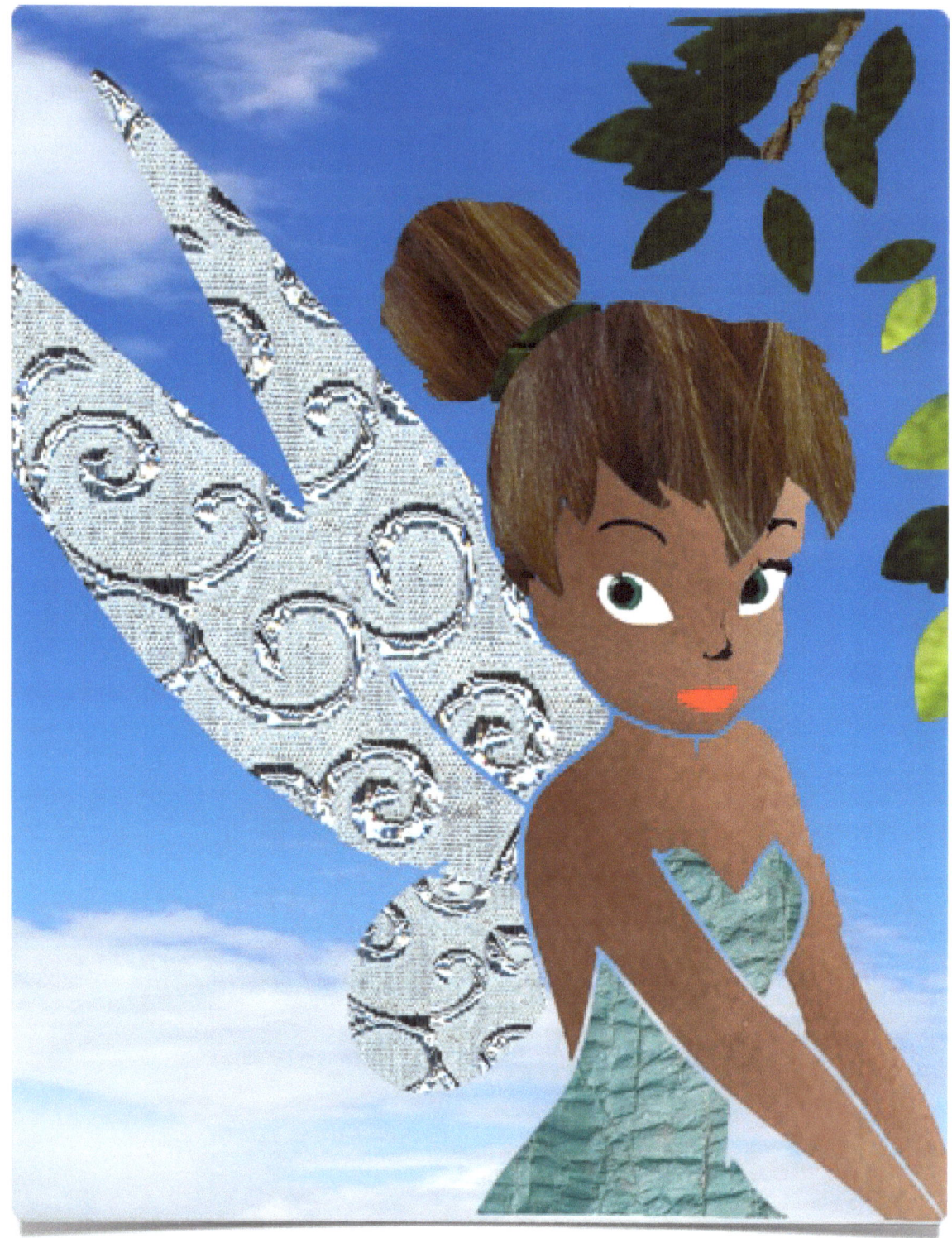

What else would Tinker-bell be? Neverland had Pirates and Native Americans.... She must be from the Caribbean!

This image is copyrighted so it is not mine

I need to be careful, so I don't get a fine.

I copied this image from a Disney coloring book,

And I made Tinker-bell Latina. It's a great look

For her and many women in all the world

Who are taught that dark skin doesn't have the allure

of Tinker-bell.

(That teaching is false, of course)

But as you can see, even dark as can be

Tinker-bell still calls to you and me

So, we can remember that because of our skin

We can and should be seen for the beauty within

Sharing Faith

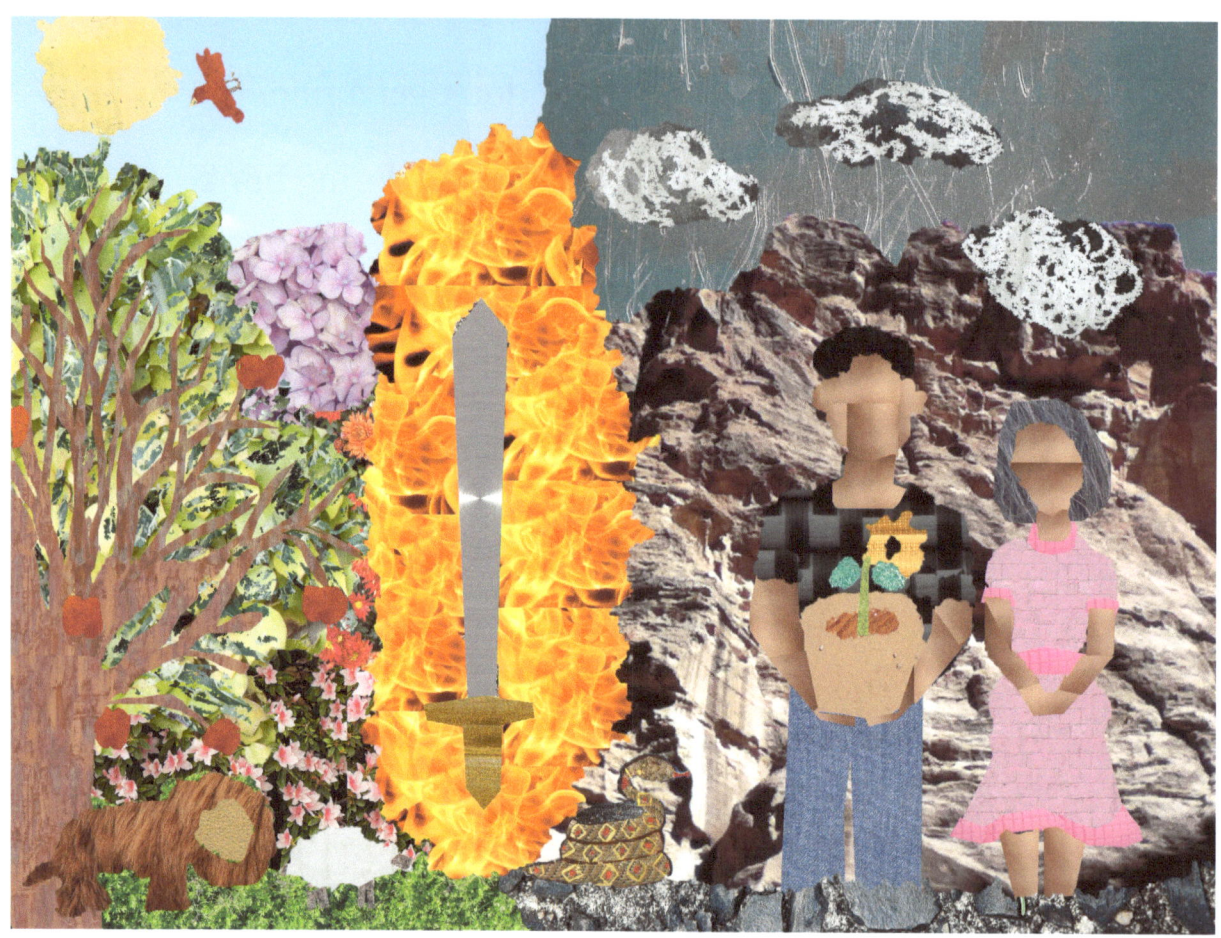

These poems are inspired by stories from the Bible and The Book of Mormon. At first, I made them to tell the stories how I saw them. But after a while, I used these stories to put in images that my children, and my nieces and nephews made. I really wanted a place to put the snake that my sister painted, so the story of Eve and Adam (Ladies first!) is pictured here.

Moses

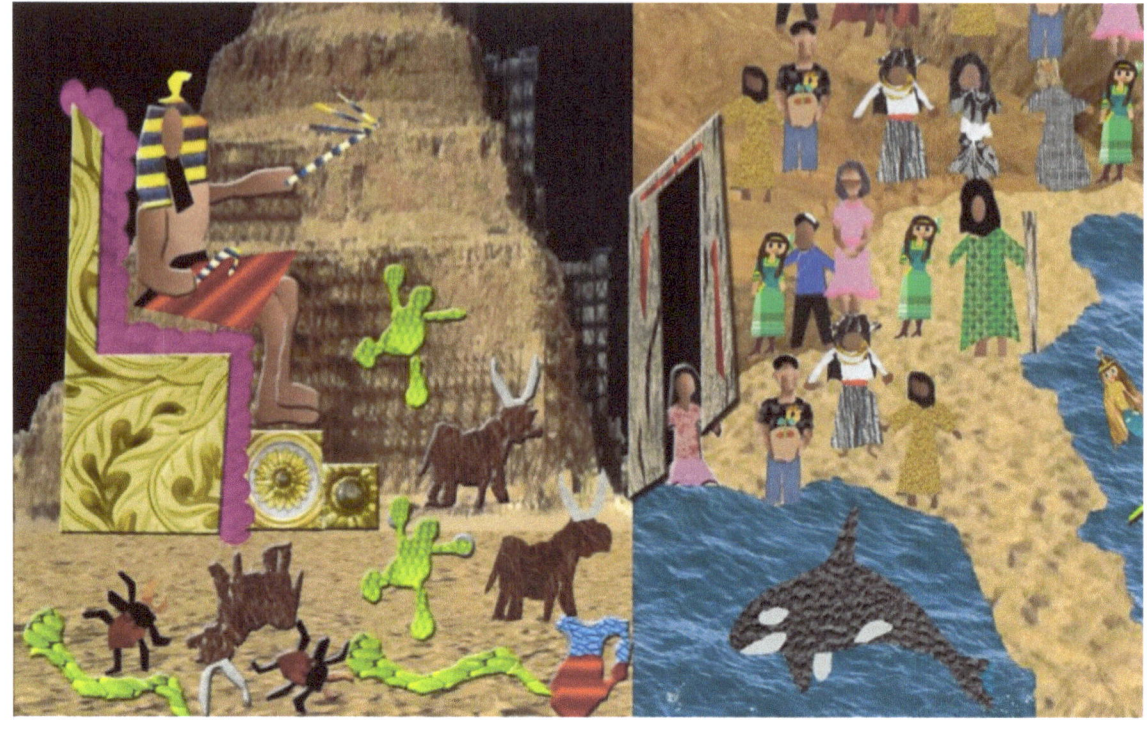

Moses was born in Egypt when his people were slaves

And they tried to get away, but the king forced them to stay

Moses escaped, then returned to get his large family

He led his nation to the desert where they could be free

Then the snakes came, and bit everyone, and they got sick

They were all dying, unless they saw the snake on the stick

Then they lived.

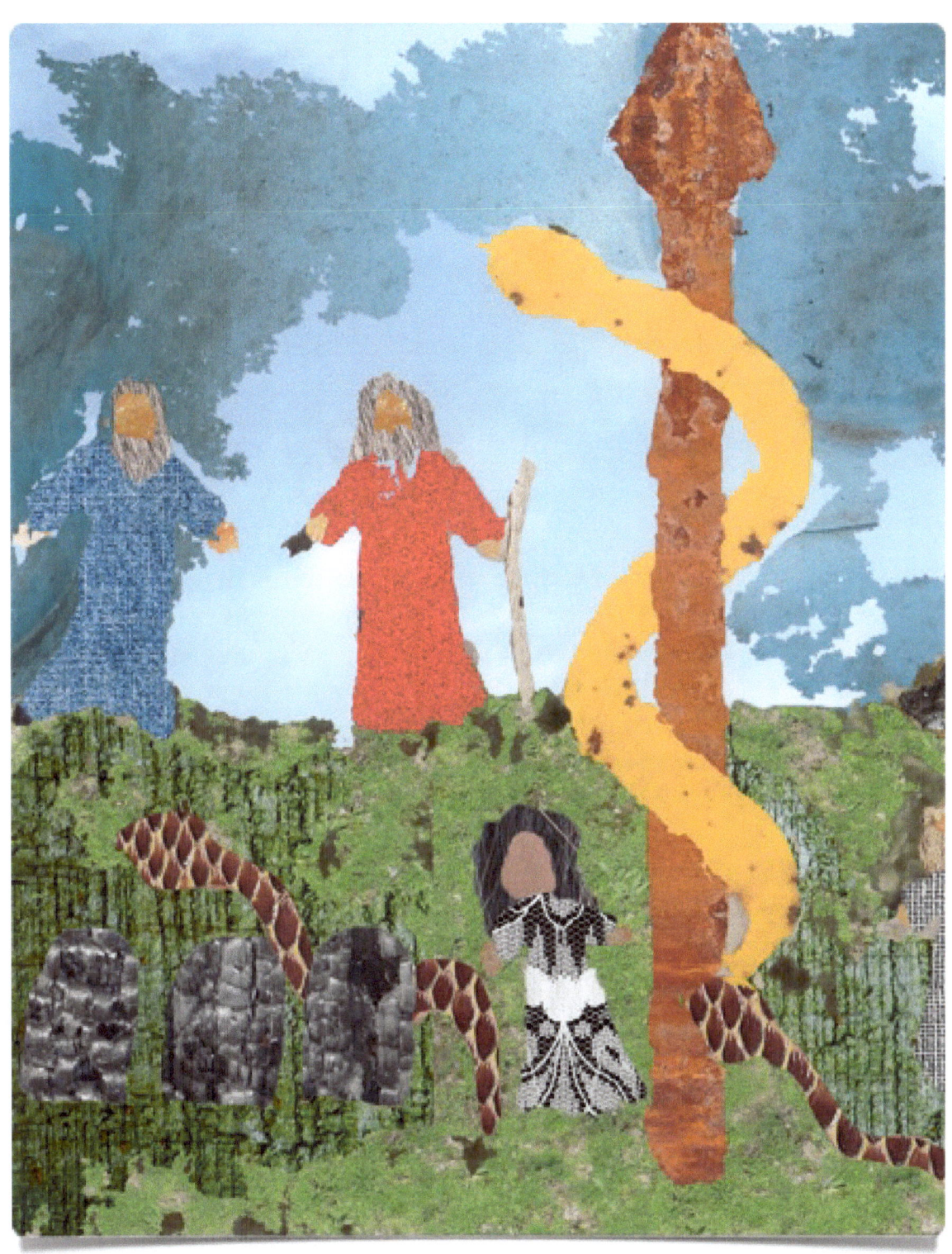

Chanukah

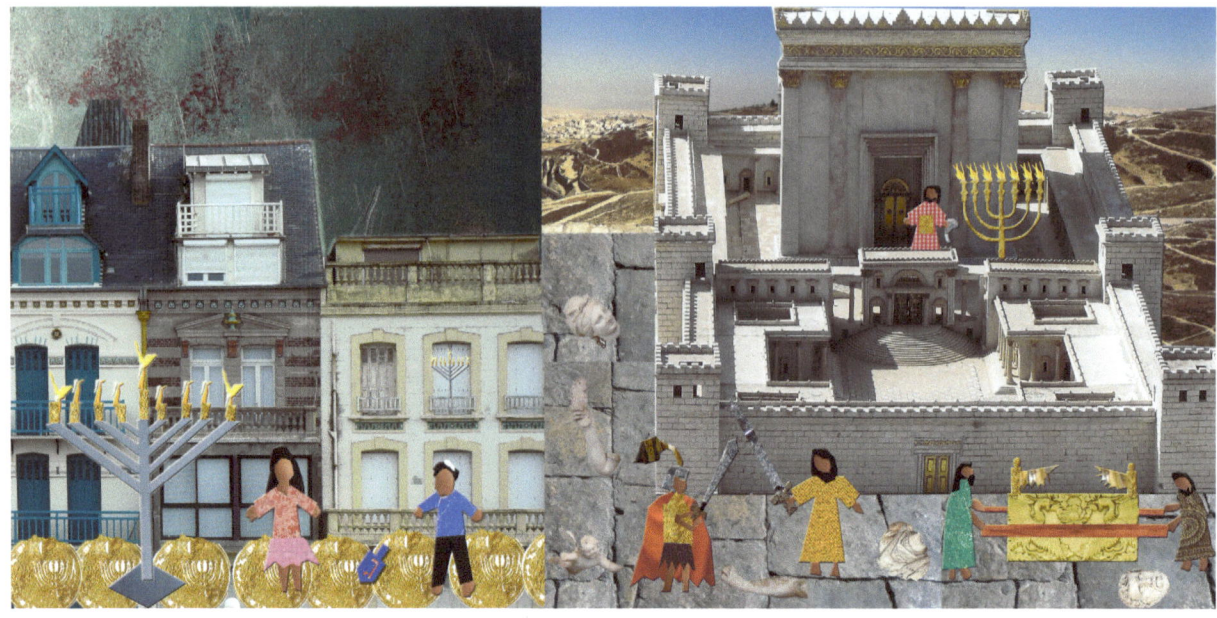

This miracle of the Maccabees is remembered today

Because of a great battle that was fought far away

The Maccabees had gotten some autonomy

From the Roman Empire, so the Romans got angry

They took over the temple and the filled it with gods

That they stole from the Greeks, (unimaginative slobs).

This offended the Jews and many others who saw

The temple as the House of their God

The priests lit the menorah with very little oil

But their God was with them, so it did not spoil

One day's worth of oil lasted one whole week

Today this miracle is remembered so that those who seek

The help of God when they are doing what's right

Can like the Maccabees, enjoy His great light.

Christmas

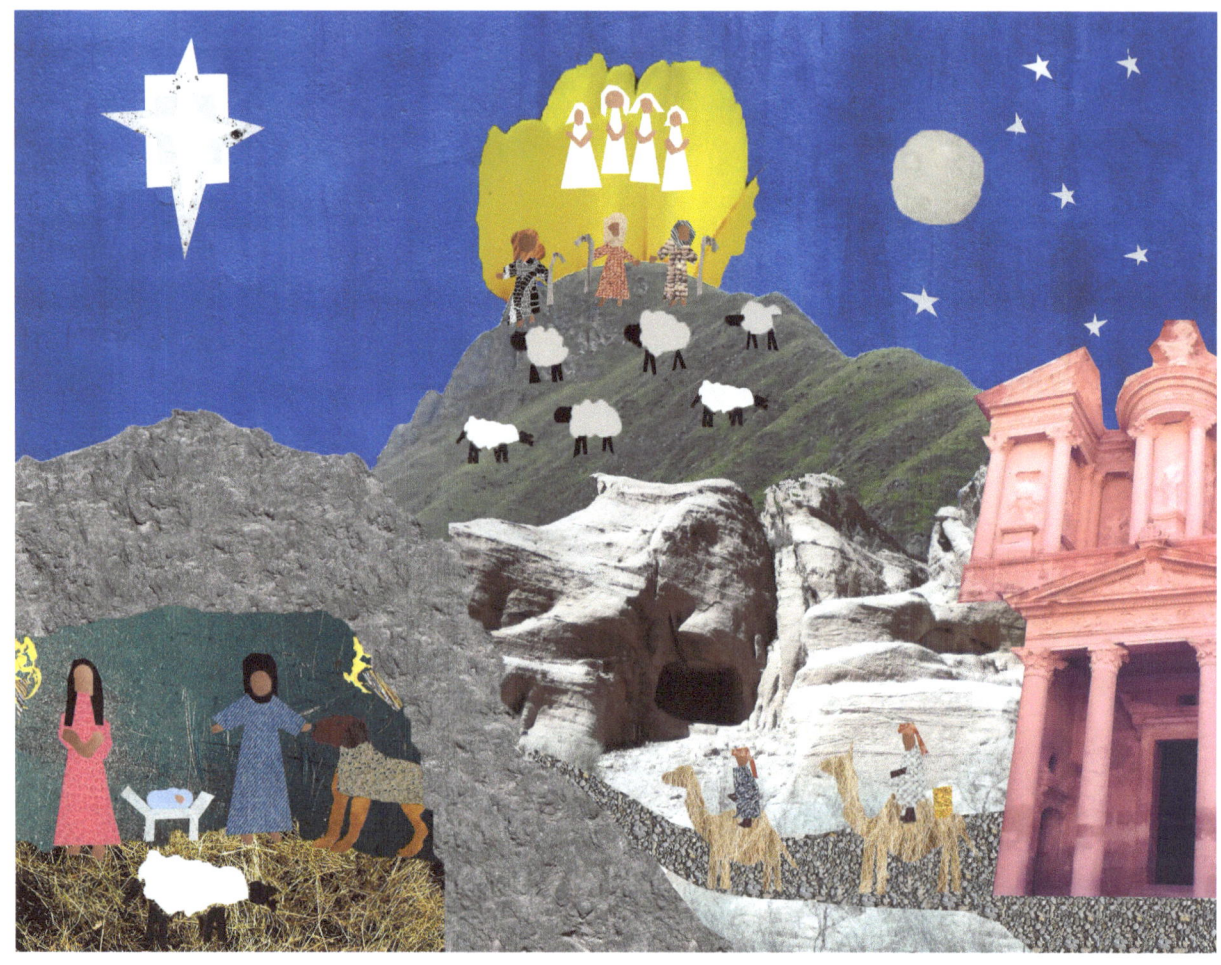

In 2011, the year our daughter was born, Moraima and I went to Israel to celebrate the 20th anniversary of our first kiss. While we were there, we took a short tour of Petra, where, to our surprise, we learned was the home of the Wise men, or the Three Kings. This is my rendition of their journey.

The wise men came to Jesus following a star

The Bible only says that they came from afar

When they arrived, they found him in a house

Much better than the cave Jesus shared with a mouse

The wise men were from Petra, across the river Jordan

Jesus now in a house, there was place to board in

The wise men gave Jesus gifts: Gold, myrrh and frankincense.

Which they changed into cash—it just made sense.

Jesus was unlucky because Herod the King

Could not stand Jesus, or the hope he would bring

Herod killed all the young boys, a horrifying act

The cash got Jesus to Egypt, He escaped that attack.

Nineveh

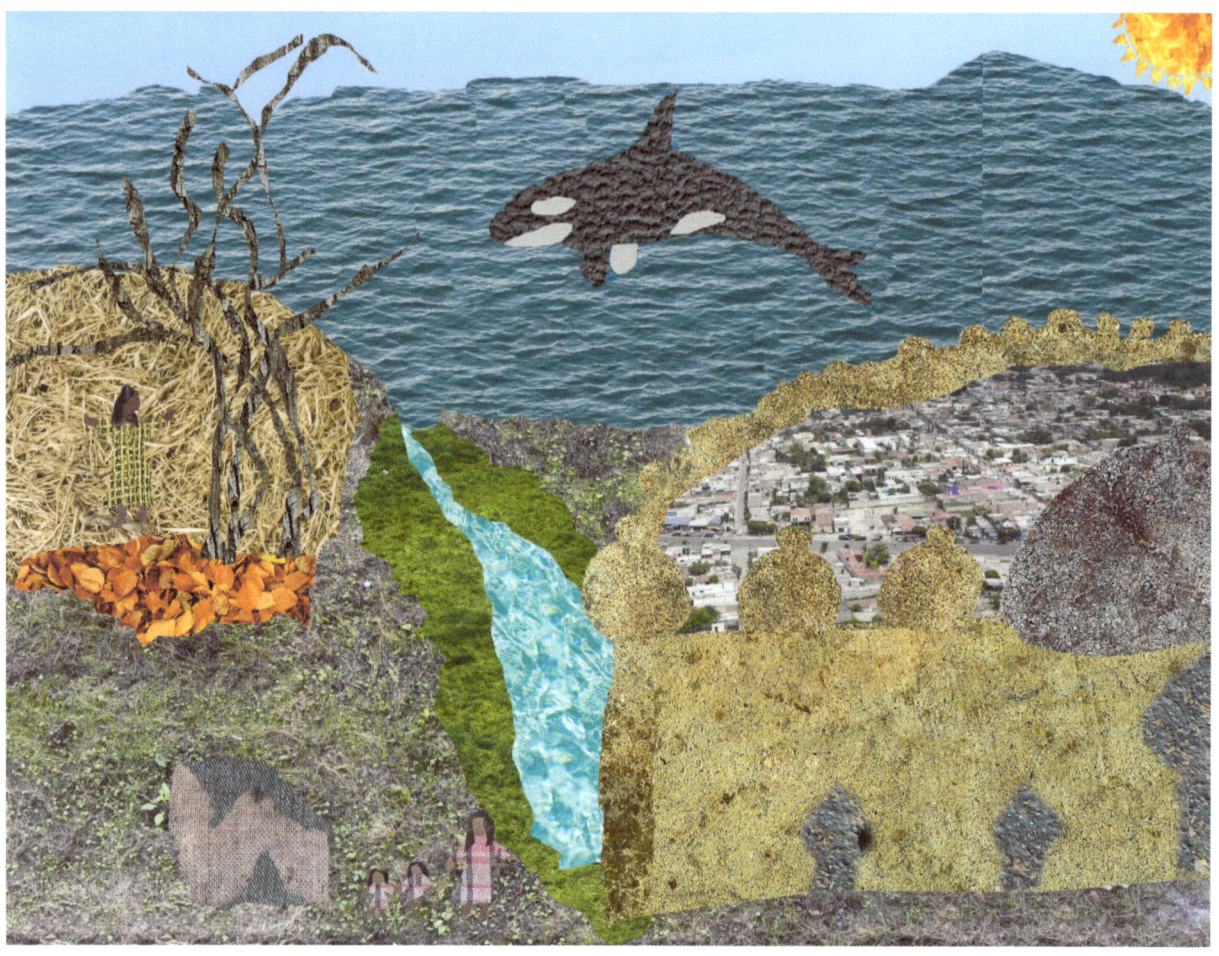

The story of Jonah always fascinated me

Because "Who would try to escape God through the sea?"

A great fish ate him and he was in it's belly three days

He was then spit up on the land to work for God's pay

He went to a wicked city, Nineveh, and preached

God decided to forgive everyone that he reached

So Jonah got mad, and he went somewhere to pout

But there was no shade and it was really hot out

He was blessed with a vine that made some excellent shade

And all of that day he relaxed and he prayed

The next day the vine died, and Jonah got hot

He got angry again; but it was all for naught

God told him that day,

"You can understand my ways,

You got sad for a tiny small vine."

"Now you know how I'd feel,

If Niniveh did not kneel

And repent; they are all children of Mine

Lehi's Dream

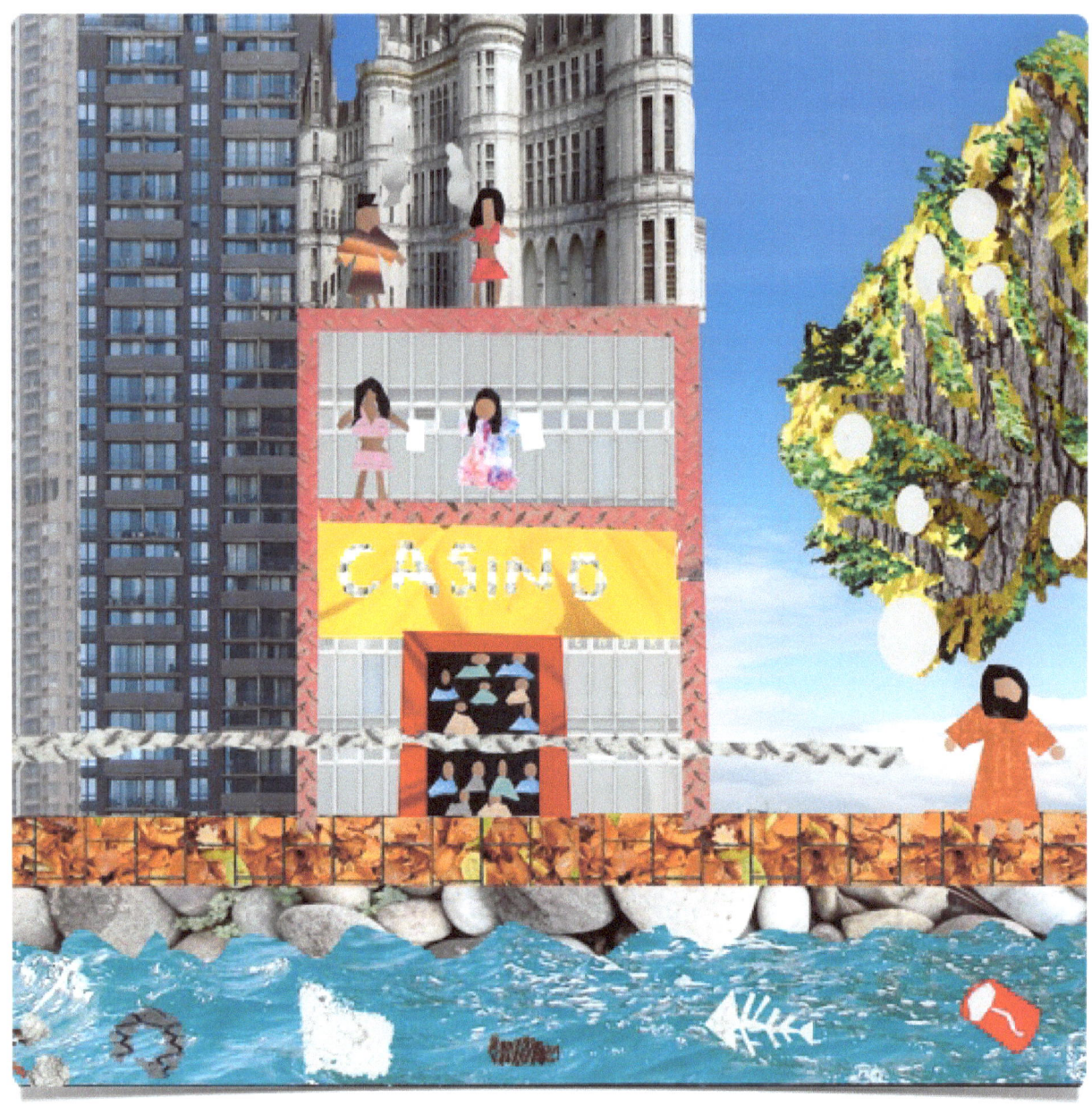

I composed this piece while trying to visualize what a great and spacious building looks like.

Lehi dreamed a dream some would call a vision

Which he would later recall with amazing precision

About a big building and a beautiful tree

That had fruit you needed to eat so you could be happy

The path was dangerous, and you could easily get lost

So, a rod of iron was provided, it was well worth the cost

As long as you held on you could get to the tree

And enjoy eternal happiness with your family

Eve and Adam

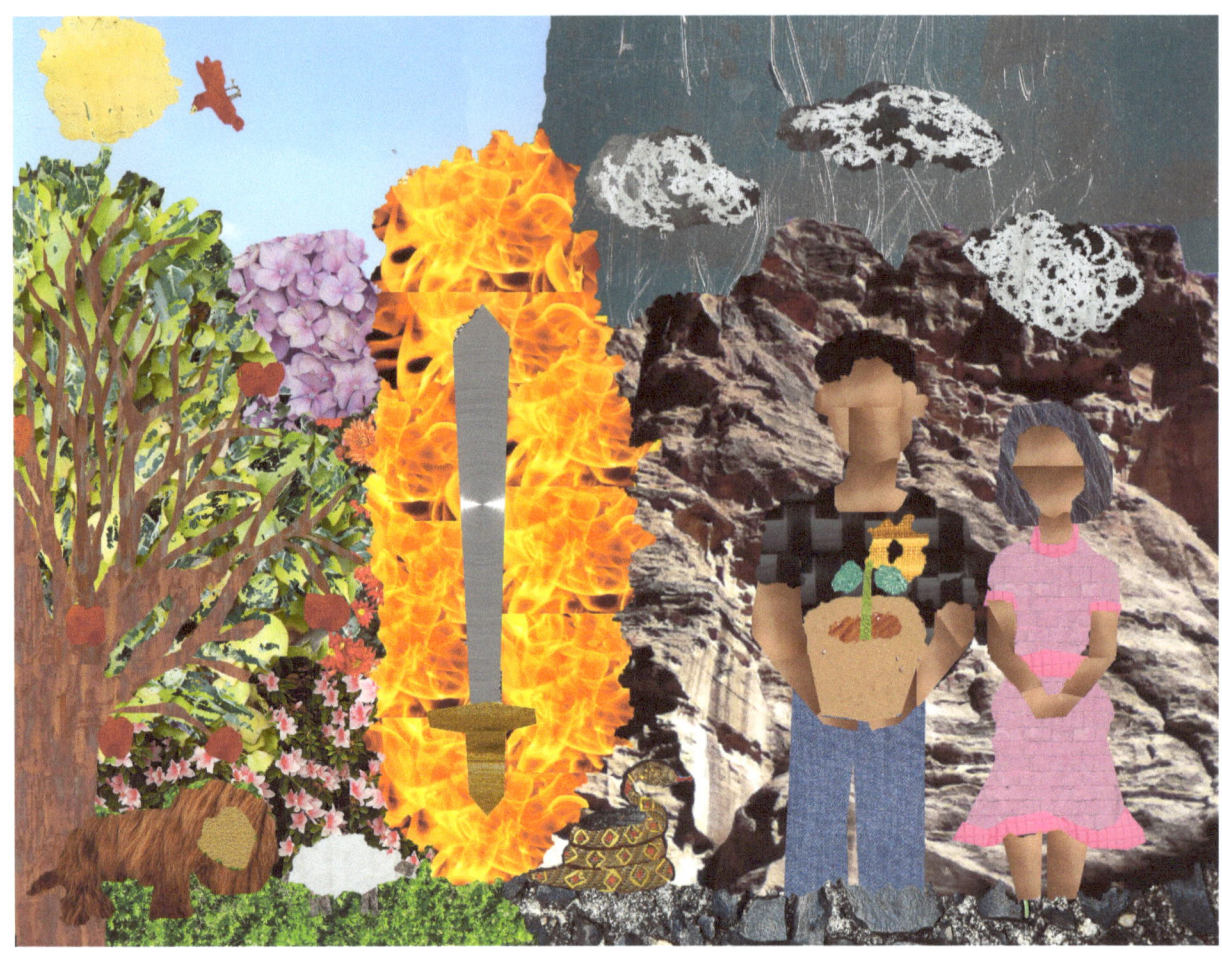

I enjoy this story of the creation of human-kind. I always felt like Eve got a bum rap, and the blame for the problems in our world in this story. I changed the name to Eve and Adam, (ladies first!) to also show that Eve led the way. She had vision at a time that her husband did not. Sound familiar?

Eve and Adam lived in paradise, made by their parents

They had a fantastic place, and they didn't pay rent

They were told they could stay as long as they ate well

But they didn't always listen and as you can tell

They ate something bad and lost their place

In paradise

They were invited to leave, and they then had to work

Taking care of the earth and start giving birth

To the human race and all of its problems

And make a life for that family, a task that was awesome

Humanity has suffered a lot, and has also experienced grace

But life's nice.

Love Everlasting

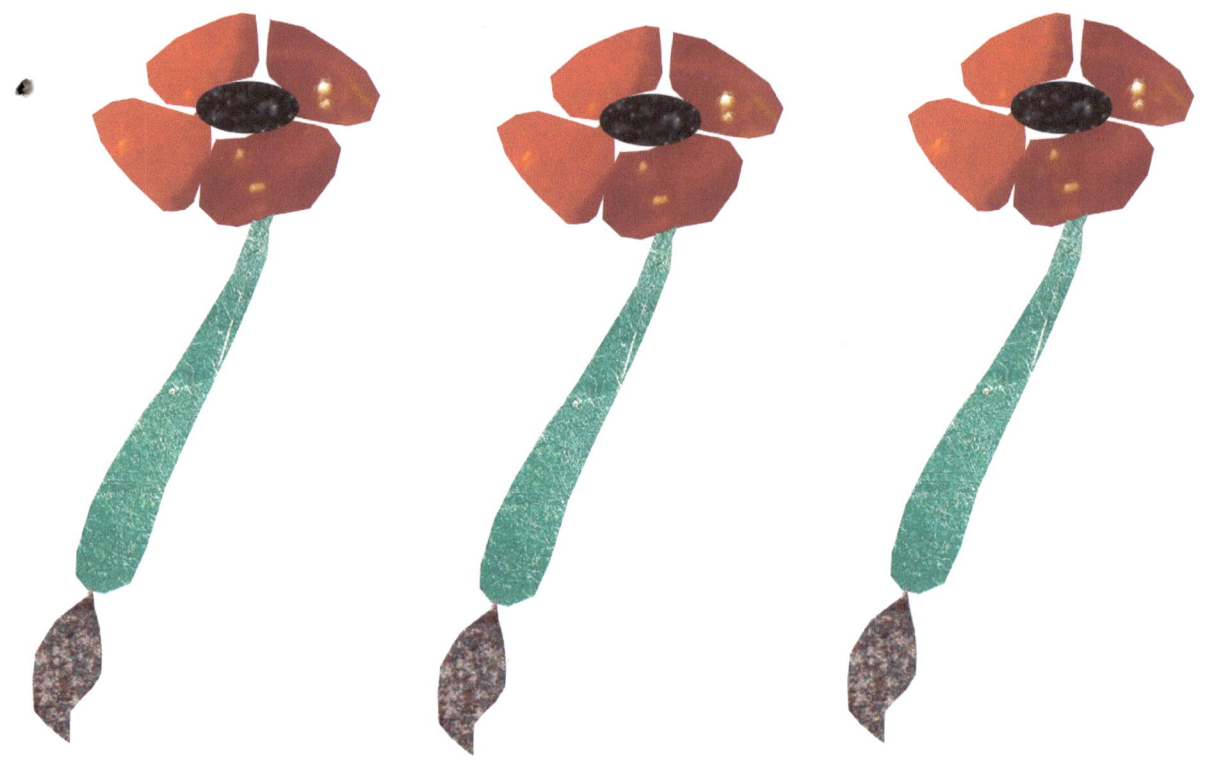

My wife Moraima has been my muse and the love of my life for three decades. These are all poems inspired by her goodness and greatness.

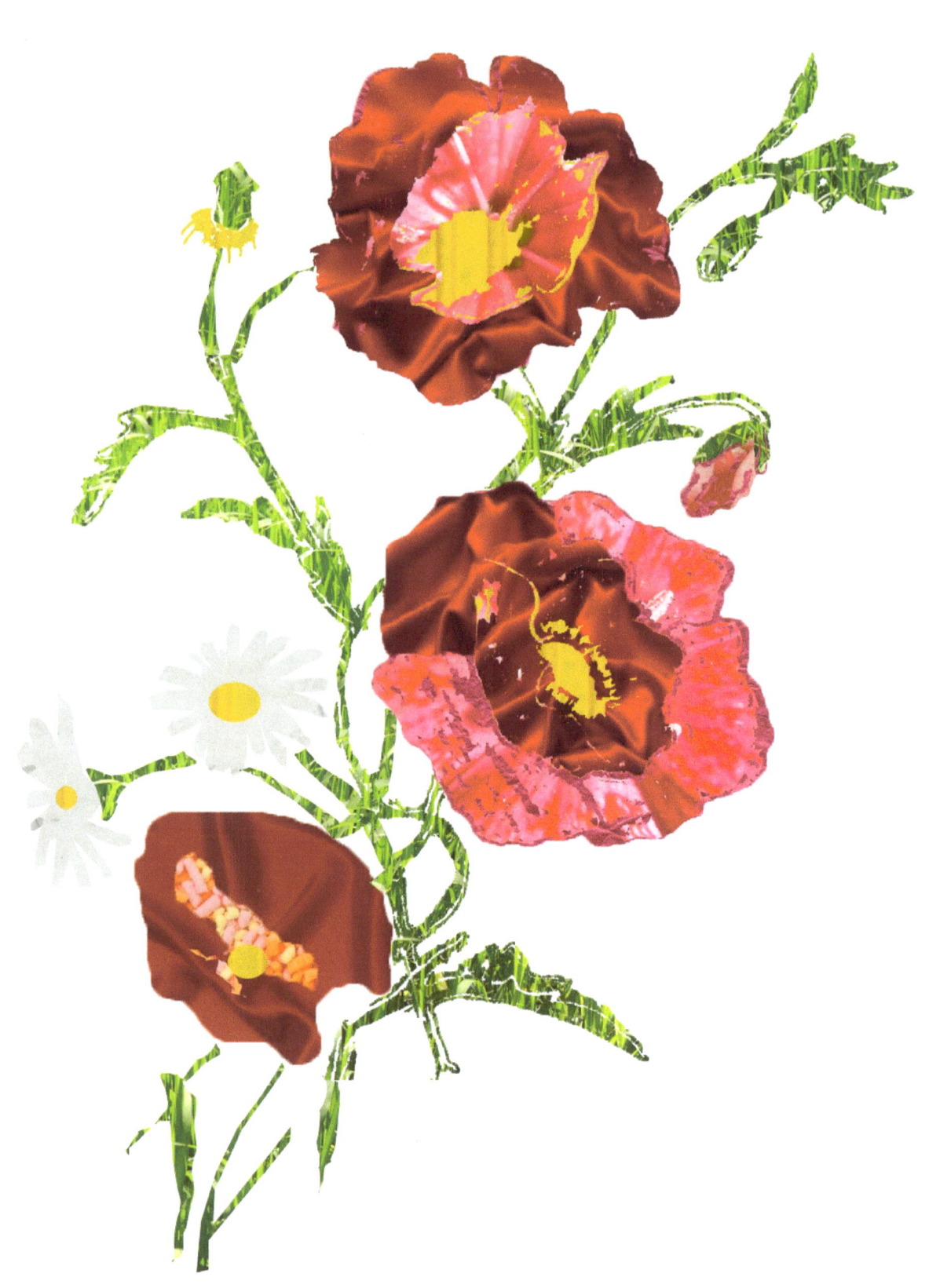

I would paint you a picture

I would paint you a picture in bright flashy colors

I would write you a story, about a time shared by lovers.

I would sing you a song, but my words can't transmit

The feelings inside me, they just would not fit.

I am lucky, no blessed, to have loved you so long

Our love, like your heart, is a beautiful song.

I have struggled to find a more personal gift,

And I hope that this poem, might give you a lift.

Your patience, your virtue, your selfless love

Reminds the whole world of what life's like up above.

You never ask for anything, always wanting to give;

Your essence, your kindness inspires others to live.

This Valentine's Day, though I might seem distant,

You will know, without doubt, I love you every instant.

Every second, every minute, every passing hour

I love you, Moraima, my most beautiful flower.

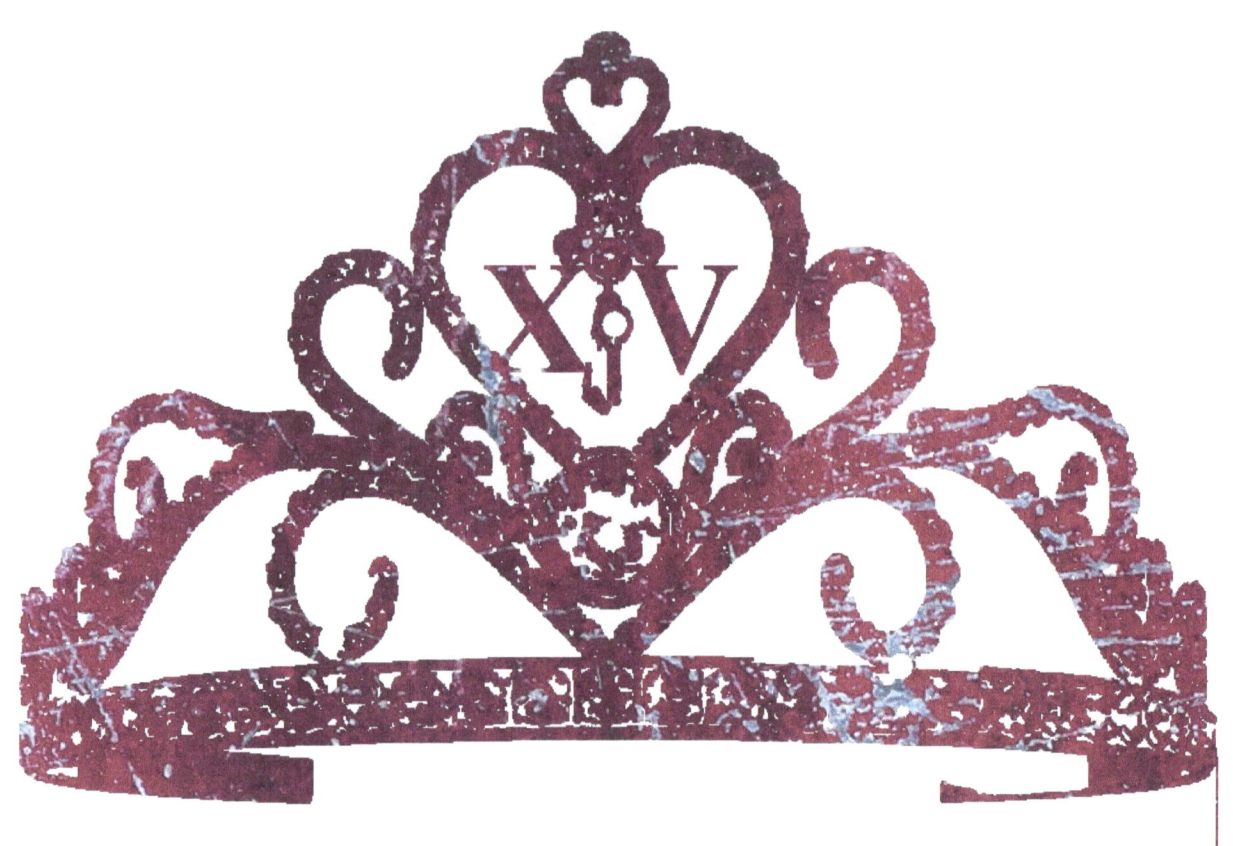

Mi Quinceañera

Fifteen years of happiness

Fifteen years of joys

Fifteen years of laughter

Fourteen of them with our boy(s)

You've changed my life completely

Fixed my attitude, cured my doubts, set me free

As I watch from a short but safe distance

I see you change eternity

I know that when you turned fifteen

Your quince was not celebrated

But you will always be my quinceañera

A fact that cannot be debated

So maybe we won't have your quince

Yet I know you'd look great in that dress

With the new high heels, and the expensive jewels

But I know big parties can stress

These first fifteen years of marriage

Will be hard, maybe impossible to beat

With you I have felt and experienced

Love's purest joys, exquisitely sweet

I pray that when our daughter arrives—

The little girl who will soon bless our home

A child that would change our family

As she joins us, to make us her own—

I have only one wish for our daughter

A small dream of what she can do

I hope that when she turns quince

She will have grown up to be just like you

www.ingramcontent.com/pod-product-compliance
Lightning Source LLC
Chambersburg PA
CBHW051216220526
45473CB00003B/1048